PONTIFICAL COUNCIL FOR JUSTICE AND PEACE

JUSTICE AND PEACE

AN EVER PRESENT CHALLENGE

LIBRERIA EDITRICE VATICANA

VATICAN CITY 2004

ISBN 88-209-7628-5

www.libreriaeditricevaticana.com

VATICAN PRESS

CONTENTS

Presentation 5

PART I. *A Look at History*

Witness to a Genesis (Card. R. Etchegaray). 9
Commitment to Justice (Card. J. M. Mejía) 12
The Defence and Promotion of Human Rights (Archbishop
A. Cordero Lanza di Montezemolo) 20
The Relationships of the Pontifical Council for Justice and
Peace with the Local Churches (Bishop W. F. Murphy) . 24
Ecumenical Collaboration in the Social Field (Sr. M. Keenan,
RSHM) 31

PART II. *A Deepening of Themes of Our Day*

Social Development and the Fight Against Poverty (Prof.
L. Sabourin) 43
Human Rights and the Dignity of the Person (Prof. M. A.
Glendon). 59
Democracy, Human Rights and the Rule of Law: the "Trin-
ity of Politics" (Prof. J. Haaland Matlary) 70
The Church's Social Teaching and the International Labour
Organization's "Decent Work" Strategy (Ambassador
J. Somavía). 84
Safeguarding the Environment (Prof. E. Barbieri Masini) . 110

PART III. *Future Prospects*

The Church's Social Doctrine in Today's World (Bishop
G. Crepaldi). 125
Ecumenical and Interreligious Dialogue at the Service of
Justice and Peace (Card. W. Kasper). 138
The Spirituality of Peace (Card. B. Gantin). 145

PRESENTATION

This publication of the Pontifical Council for Justice and Peace, in process for some time, comes on the eve of two important events. At the end of this year, in October 2004, the "First World Congress of Ecclesial Organizations Working for Justice and Peace" will be held, and the 40th anniversary of the Pastoral Constitution *Gaudium et Spes* will be celebrated next year.

These two events are of great importance to this Dicastery which, while basing its roots in the conciliar document calling for its institution, finds in the organisms created by the local Episcopal Conferences the most appropriate interlocutors in the common task to "arouse the Catholic community to foster progress in needy regions and social justice among nations" (*Gaudium et Spes*, No. 90).

It seems, therefore, the opportune moment to impart a "new dynamism" to the Pontifical Council as well as to social-pastoral in general. This volume was conceived as an instrument for such a purpose, reflecting what the Holy Father wrote at the beginning of the Letter *Novo Millennio Ineunte*, namely "to remember the past" in order "to live the present with enthusiasm and to look forward to the future with confidence".

In the part dedicated to *a look at history*, some of the main actors of the first thirty years of the existence of the Pontifical Council were asked to contribute their reflections. In addition to the witness of their activity in some of the areas of interest of the Dicastery, living personal memories have been interwoven to recall the times during which the principle commitment was to reaffirm the validity of the Church's social doctrine as an instrument of evangelization. My venerated predecessor, Cardinal François-Xavier Nguyên Van Thuân, to whom we owe the inspiration of this volume and whom the Lord called home two years ago, devoted himself to this commitment with special attention to the particular churches outside of Europe.

In the second part, some noted personalities of the academic and international world have deepened what have been singled out as the most *important themes of our day*. These personalities, in addition to being specialists in their respective disciplines, are very familiar to the Pontifical Council for Justice and Peace, owing to the collaboration that they have lent and continue to lend in various capacities.

The third and final part looks to *future prospects* in a progression that seemed most appropriate. From a study on the fundamental core of the

Dicastery, that is, the social doctrine of the Church and its place in the world of today and tomorrow, we arrive to a reflection on one of the most problematic future challenges for globalized humanity: religious dialogue as an instrument at the service of justice and peace to be undertaken with a renewed ecumenical sentiment. This third part, and the volume itself, concludes with a close examination of the theme of peace by Cardinal Bernardin Gantin, who was a Council Father at Vatican II and the first President of the Pontifical Council for Justice and Peace after it received its definitive mandate from Pope Paul VI.

My wish is that this publication, conceived with the temporal vision just described, may contribute to renewing hope and pushing Christians to set out adventurously also on the ethical and social path that is an essential dimension of Christian witness (cf. *Novo Millennio Ineunte*, No. 52): *Duc in altum*!

RENATO RAFFAELE Card. MARTINO
President of the Pontifical Council for Justice and Peace

PART I

A Look at History

WITNESS TO A GENESIS...

Cardinal ROGER ETCHEGARAY *

When I wish to get to know someone well, I try to discover his roots, even to make a visit to his birthplace if possible. The same is true for an institution: its "genesis" brings its vocation fully into view and enables one to grasp better its destiny. Well, the Pontifical Council for Justice and Peace is the legitimate child of the Second Vatican Council. The official acts of the Council prove this quite readily and, were it necessary, I myself could testify to this, since I was present in Saint Peter's Basilica in Rome on 7 December 1965, when the Council Fathers came up with the idea for this Council in voting on the Pastoral Constitution *Gaudium et Spes*. This text, the last to be promulgated, carries the significant title: "The Church in the Modern World"; and in No. 90, just before the document's conclusion, it expresses the following wish: "Considering the immense hardships which still afflict the majority of men and women today, the Council regards it as most opportune that some Department of the universal Church be set up for the worldwide promotion of justice for the poor and of Christ's love for them. The role of such an organism would be to stimulate the Catholic community to foster progress in needy regions and social justice among nations".

There are other Roman Dicasteries that can claim the honour of being spiritual heirs of *Gaudium et Spes*, but the Dicastery for Justice and Peace is the only one that is truly the fruit of its bosom.

During the third session of 1964, while debate was under way on what was then called "Schema XIII", the idea was advanced of asking the Pope to create a study and promotion Department for dealing with issues of development and social justice. The very first voice raised in this regard at the Council was that of Father Gerald Mahon, Superior General of the Mill Hill Missionaries (Great Britain). He was the spokesman for a group of Bishops and experts among whom I must cite three Americans whom I came to know well: Monsignor Joseph Gremillion, of Catholic Relief Services; Monsignor Luigi Ligutti, the Holy See's Observer at the Food and Agriculture Organization of the UN; and James Norris, a lay auditor at the Council. But

---

* President of the Pontifical Council for Justice and Peace from 1984 to 1998.

neither can I forget the meetings of Bishops regarding "the Church of the poor", which took place at the Belgian College led by the Most Reverend Himmer, Bishop of Tournai, and the Most Reverend Mercier, Bishop of Laghouat in southern Algeria, with the presence also of an Eastern Christian, in the person of the Greek-Melkite Patriarch Maximos IV. Between the third and fourth sessions, at the prompting of a Mill Hill Missionary, Arthur McCormack, a long note was drafted explaining the motivation for requesting a Roman "secretariat" and increasing the chances of viability by suggesting a series of concrete programmes. This note, translated into several languages, was distributed unofficially to the Council Fathers at the beginning of the fourth session.

At the time of the last debate on "Schema XIII" (4-5 October 1965), at least eight Council Fathers took up anew the idea of a secretariat: it was not clear what its precise duties would be, but one of its fundamental tasks would be the fight against poverty, a factor contributing to inequalities and conflicts in the world. Among these interventions, Father Mahon again took up the lead, forcefully supporting the Most Reverend Angelo Fernandes, Archbishop of New Delhi. Another defence of this idea coming from the Third World was that of Cardinal McCann, Archbishop of Cape Town, who himself recounted to me — one day when I went to visit him in South Africa — how his intervention was greeted with great and unexpected enthusiasm. It was 5 October, and the morning was drawing to an end: he was the last to speak, not only in the presence of the Council Fathers but also of the Diplomatic Corps which had been convoked at Saint Peter's to welcome Pope Paul VI back from New York where he had made his historic visit to the United Nations on 4 October. The Pope's speech to the United Nations, which still has an urgent relevance today, was relayed to Saint Peter's with a fervour that still rings in my ears. Recalling his message of peace addressed to the UN Assembly, the Pontiff told us: "Never has the mission of the Church, mediator between God and man, been justified by a more evident, more providential, more modern rationale... We must consequently examine and apply our programmes with increased vigour, for we have made an appeal for peace as the goal towards which all of us must work today: may God grant that to our witness of words there be added our witness of action".

This helps us to understand better what happened next. The Council closed on 8 December, preciously carrying away within its bosom paragraph No. 90 of *Gaudium et Spes*, which was quoted at the beginning of this presentation. What did Pope Paul VI do about this? After having heard him upon his return from the UN, no one could doubt that he would honour, and quickly so, the request of the Council Fathers. Making this a reality was not so simple for those inside the Vatican, where another decision of the Council, concerning the creation of a Department for the apostolate of the laity, crossed the same path. Under the leadership of Monsignor Benelli (who would a year later become Substitute of the Secretariat of State) a work-group composed of twenty people — among whom Vittorino Veronese (a colloquium analyzing the effective role of this "layman in the Church and in the world" took place on 7-8 May 1993, with particularly reference to the origins of the Roman Dicastery for Justice and Peace; cf. GIORGIO FILIBECK, *Vittorino Veronese: un cristiano al servizio della giustizia e della pace*, in *Vittorino Veronese, un laico nella chiesa e nel mondo*, Ed. A.V.E., Roma 1994, pp. 135-136) — met at the Columbus Hotel from 9 to 12 May 1966.

Being obliged to stay within the limits of a personal testimony, I shall end here my brief contribution. On 6 January 1967, with the Motu Proprio *Catholicam Christi Ecclesiam*, Pope Paul VI instituted two Departments, the Council for the Laity and the Pontifical Commission for Justice and Peace, and entrusted to Cardinal Maurice Roy, the Archbishop of Quebec, the joint responsibility for both. The Pontifical Commission underwent two experimental periods: the first, from 1967 to 1971, guided by the Encyclical *Populorum Progressio* and the Apostolic Letter *Octogesima Adveniens*, and the second, from 1971 to 1976, helping out with the Synod on "Justice in the World". In the end, the definitive mandate was given (10 December 1976).

From 1984 to 1998, without of course having imagined anything of the kind at the time of its pre-history in the Council, I found myself, by the grace of Pope John Paul II, at the head, or rather at the heart of this beautiful ship... but that is another... story! It is not my place to turn those pages here, except to thank God, and all those who embarked with me on this same apostolic adventure! I was very happy to sail on an ark that carried a biblical name: "justice and peace will kiss" (*Ps* 85:10).

October 2002

COMMITMENT TO JUSTICE

Cardinal JORGE M. MEJÍA *

The contribution that I was asked to make to this volume belongs to its first part, that is to the historical section. To attempt, however, even a brief review of the work carried out by the Dicastery during these past 35 years in the area of "justice", the first term of its twofold title, runs the risk of being purely descriptive or even merely trite. Who can list all that the Dicastery has done to promote justice, in one way or another, either on its own initiative or indirectly? Such a range of questions related to justice come to my mind for the period during which I was Vice President — at the request of Pope John Paul II and under the guidance and direction of Cardinal Roger Etchegaray — that it is difficult to decide where to begin. Perhaps I should start with the meeting with UNITA rebels in Angola to try to convince them that the path they had chosen was a dead-end and that terrorism served no purpose, despite the equally destructive tendencies of their adversaries who were firmly in control of the country. Or I could begin with that working lunch with directors of the World Bank to present our then-recently-published document on the foreign debt. Or still again, with the various meetings with the Holy Father in preparation for the World Day of Prayer for Peace held in Assisi on 27 October 1986. Yes, I could, but then it could be argued that I was entering into the domain of the other term in the title: "peace". Yet who is able to distinguish between the two terms precisely? And who could have done so on the specific occasion of the second World Day of Prayer held in Assisi on January 26, 2002? Who could do so now?

The fact is that, on the one hand, the two aspects of the dual title were not brought together simply to form a whole, so as not to leave anything out. On the other hand, moreover, justice, if it is considered the name of a virtue, is — as traditionally taught — a universal virtue, one of those virtues that embrace in one way or other all of human activity. Moreover, the profound and inseparable unity of the twofold title "Justice and Peace" comes from Sacred Scripture, which has always joined them, and not only in Psalm 85 (verse 11). In fact, the one cannot exist without the other: neither peace

---

* Vice-President of the Pontifical Council for Justice and Peace from 1986 to 1994.

without justice, nor justice without peace. In reality, if the first formulation is generally accepted, the same cannot always be said for the second. Yet the work, that is its mandate and mission, was entrusted to the Dicastery by the prophetic vision of the Second Vatican Council (*Gaudium et Spes*, No. 90) and the no less prophetic decision of Paul VI, first in the Motu Proprio *Catholicam Christi Ecclesiam* of 6 January 1967, and then in the Motu Proprio *Justitiam et Pacem* of 10 December 1976 which established the Dicastery in its definitive form. Its duty is precisely to keep them firmly together, both in the teaching of the Social Doctrine of the Church and in any practical suggestions offered to the community of the faithful as well as to men and women of good will. It is difficult, therefore, to speak of justice in the work of the Dicastery without including its commitment to peace and vice-versa.

How, therefore, shall I present this overview? It would be possible to follow two or three more or less parallel paths, which, in the end, would largely cover the commitment of the Pontifical Council, if not during its more than 35 years of existence, at least for the period of my service (1986-1994) and perhaps beyond.

The first path is that of teaching, or better still, of witness. If it is true that every commitment of a Dicastery of the Holy See, especially one specifically dedicated to teaching, has a witness value vis-à-vis Christian truth and, indeed, the person of Christ, then certainly the principal commitment of Justice and Peace, according to the previously cited Motu Proprio *Justitiam et Pacem* (art. II, 1), is the deepening and the diffusion of the Social Doctrine of the Church. In doing so, it gives witness to the meaning and content, as well as to the obligatory nature, of this Doctrine. It is not so much a question of a theoretical teaching as of a teaching oriented towards action. Above all, it is perhaps a question of clearly affirming the relationship between putting social teachings into practice and faithfulness to evangelical exigencies.

The work of the Dicastery has been immense in this field. We need only think of the various official documents published in recent years. I have already mentioned that on the foreign debt: *At the Service of the Human Community. An Ethical Approach to the International Debt Question*. Mention must also be made of the documents on the housing problem, on the international arms trade, on agrarian reform, as well as that very important and still timely on *The Church and Racism*. And this is not all. I believe that it is clear to all that the Pontifical Council for Justice and Peace plays an important role in the preparation of the annual Messages for the celebration of the World Day of Peace, the first of which was held in 1968. After a serious attempt has been made to identify a pressing issue, the Message is prepared in close collaboration with the Holy Father. Its central theme is, of course, one or another aspect of peace. As noted above, however, there is not a single Message in which the inseparable exigencies of justice are not carefully brought out. It suffices to go through the themes of each Message in a publication of the Pontifical Council, *Ways of Peace* (a collection of the Messages from 1968 to 1986).

This leads us to speak of other publications of "*Justitia et Pax*". The list is highly rich and varied in titles, yet always within the framework of the Social Teaching, and consequently the requirements of justice. I will mention only the more recent: the volume by Dr. Giorgio Filibeck on the teaching of the last Pontiffs in the area of human rights (*Human Rights in the Teaching of the Church: from John XXIII to John Paul II*). The centrality of justice and the extent of its applies are clearly brought out. What actually are human rights, if correctly understood, if not the manifestation of justice towards oneself and towards others and, above all, the indication of the limits beyond which a society that seeks, precisely, to be just towards its members cannot go?

Unfortunately, when this "reflection-recollection" was written in April 2002, the major document on the Social Doctrine, originally and provisionally entitled *Compendium*, had not yet been published. In a certain sense, this document, dedicated to the complete and systematic presentation of the Church's Social Doctrine, will once again have justice not so much as a key theme but as the necessary boundaries of personal and social conduct inspired by the Gospel and the tradition of the Social Teaching of the Church: that is, as already noted, justice as an all-embracing virtue.

A teaching that has witness value is not, however, limited by any means to documents and other publications. It is a constant activity of the Pontifical Council, and this in two principal ways. I am thinking above all of the presence of the superiors but also of the officials (to whom — which it is likewise just to recognize — the Dicastery owes much, both to the present officials as to those who preceded them) at meetings of various international or regional organizations where the Holy See is often represented by the Dicastery. I referred above to my presence at a working lunch of the World Bank on the occasion of the publication of the document on foreign debt. This was certainly not an isolated episode. In each of these challenging and important circumstances, I always tried to emphasize the need for international justice, particularly on the economic level. I must say that I always, or almost always, found an attentive ear and sincere openness. Archbishop Diarmuid Martin, current Representative of the Holy See to the International Organizations in Geneva — but in my time Under-Secretary of the

Dicastery — could enrich this chapter with his personal experience.[1] We may briefly recall his participation in the major international conferences of the United Nations on the environment, women, poverty, and so forth. The superiors were not the only ones to carry out these delicate functions. I am thinking of the presentations of Dr. Filibeck at the San Remo sessions on humanitarian law, and of Dr. Giovanelli at more than one regional meeting of National "Justice and Peace" Commissions, and so forth.

Through this participation, with its related public presentations, and direct personal contacts, what was accomplished if not a witnessing to the needs of justice in the many areas of human action and in various situations that are often difficult if not dramatic? Once again, we see justice as a universal virtue.

Most recently, economic justice or, if one wishes, justice in economic relations, both within each nation or region and internationally — which, as is well-known, are closely related — occupies a privileged place, even if the word "privileged" might not be the most adequate expression. The Holy Father has been, and is particularly concerned, because in this area there still remains the unresolved question about the gap, or better still the abyss, between the world of the rich and the world of the poor; between development or over-development, to adopt an expression from the encyclical *Sollicitudo Rei Socialis*, and under-development; between leisure time and unemployment, and so forth. His three major social encyclicals are related to the work of the Dicastery, from the first one of 1981 (*Laborem Exercens*) to the last of 1991 (*Centesimus Annus*), together with the previously mentioned *Sollicitudo Rei Socialis* of 1988. This is not only because the themes developed are part of the Social Teaching of the Church. The Pope called upon the contribution of the Dicastery in the preparation of these documents, asking, among others, Cardinal Etchegaray and the author of these pages to verify how the economic world perceived the problems related to international economic justice, even at the level of international financial organizations. The aim was to keep their understanding of them in mind in the magisterial reflection on these problems. Two meetings were held with renowned representatives of various branches of the economic sciences. The Dicastery later published their presentations in two volumes. However, what is perhaps less well known is that the Holy Father wanted to talk with them during lunch. Not only did he listen to them but also expressed his opinion. In a certain sense, *Centesimus Annus* goes back over the same or similar questions as

---

[1] Archbishop Martin has since been named Coadjutor, with right of succession, of the Cardinal-Archbishop of Dublin.

those addressed during the above-mentioned meetings, from the point of view of the Social Doctrine. It therefore ended up by becoming a veritable document of the Magisterium. There was a true dialogue, which, I hope, has never been interrupted. On the part of "*Justitia et Pax*", therefore, a common search for justice in the economic realm and, at the same time, a strong witness to justice according to the natural law but likewise according to the Gospel, was attained.

As said above, teaching is inseparable from witness. If this is particularly evident in examples such as those just cited, it is no less so in the almost daily meetings with those people and groups from across the world who visit the Dicastery. Such meetings are no less efficacious for their being of a less public and at times even confidential nature. In the beginning of this text, I referred to one of these meetings. There were many others. I had the impression — and I do not think I am wrong — that sometimes, at least in certain very difficult cases of internal or international conflicts, receiving the protagonists at "*Justitia et Pax*" was less visible, and therefore less demanding, than receiving these same persons or groups at the Secretariat of State. With regard to one of these meetings, I remember that the Holy Father bantered with Cardinal Etchegaray and myself, pointedly saying that: "*Justitia et Pax* is like a little Secretariat of State!". Obviously, both before and after such meetings, "*Justitia et Pax*" never failed to inform the Secretariat of State. It, in turn, furnished all the necessary information and pertinent directives. It is needless to emphasize the significance that these meetings had for us. Often flanked by our collaborators, we were called to give witness to the demands of justice, for example with regard to the use of violence as a means for solving conflicts, and also with regard to a certain necessarily (or at least inevitable) gradual approach in the application of just measures, but also, if the case required it, in regard to the requirements of a higher justice, which is ultimately that of forgiveness. Speaking with our interlocutors, who may or may not have been Catholic, we felt it a duty also to express this need. As is well known, the Holy Father made forgiveness the principal topic of his 2002 Message for the World Day of Peace, and may I repeat myself: justice and peace are intrinsically related when it is a question of this highly sensitive point as well.

It would be unjust — justice also reappears in this context — to fail to recognize how much we are indebted, at times rather unexpectedly, to the many people with whom we speak, as regards our discourse on justice, its applications, and the obstacles to overcome in putting it into practice. I am thinking above all of the *ad limina* visits of the Episcopal Conferences, which gave us a vivid appreciation of the problems of justice in their countries, together with what solutions could or could not be applied. We were attentive listeners to these testimonies and were aware — and he who writes perhaps much more than others — of how, if the needs of justice are universal and without exception, they cannot nevertheless be mechanically applied. The judgment of pastors who are daily involved in the struggle for justice and are conscious of the complexity of the problems and the fragility of the men and women entrusted to them, made us more aware, one could say, of the human dimensions of what was considered necessary to do. This was a dialogue that enriched us in the very exercise of our mission. I can and must say the same of others of various origins who came to speak with us: representatives of governments and international institutions, but also of more or less marginal movements or even those of a questionable or even faulty orientation.

The Dicastery is not comprised only of "Roman" components, the permanent staff, superiors and officials. The Holy Father periodically names so-called external members and consulters, from various parts of the world, with whom the Council meets in the Plenary Assembly every year and a half or two years, and with whom a rather continual relationship is maintained. One can easily imagine how much is owed to these persons — ecclesiastics and lay people, men and women — in increasing our awareness, and above all our sensitivity, in facing problems of justice, both within the various countries or regions and internationally. It is a learning experience that, in reality, will never end.

We still need to make a brief reference to certain declarations or public interventions that the Dicastery is requested to make to encourage a just solution to particular conflicts or to indicate the path to avoid if justice is to be respected. I remember more than one case, and I would like to set them within the general theme of witness. In addition, they also serve as an illustration of the value of justice as that universal virtue to which nothing is foreign. This leads us to appreciate the importance of the Dicastery's mission within the Roman Curia and, at the same time, to value the great responsibility that weighs on its shoulders, on the shoulders, that is, of those who comprise it at every level.

Having arrived at this point, I should not like to close this overview without looking towards the future. I should like to point out, obviously only indicatively and with all the necessary reserves since I am only one of the many members of the Dicastery, although still tied to it in many ways, some lines of study on the theme of justice, which present a special interest both from the point of view of reflection and of commitment. I will choose three of them, among others that could perhaps be listed.

A most current problem of justice is without doubt that of the so-called "just" war. Yes, it is true, the conditions of a "just" war or, if one prefers, the conditions for justice in a military conflict, have always been part of the tradition of the Church's Social Teaching. Today, however, in a climate of terrorism which has been "elevated" (if it is permissible to say so) to the level of a true and actual war, and of a "counter-terrorism" which has not paid sufficient attention to just limits — to mention only these two elements of judgment — justice in war becomes an ever more serious, and I would say almost radical, problem. Is it permissible or not, is it just or not, to wage war?

A second no less current problem is that of the justice of the punishments applied to those judged to be criminals by society and, in the first place, the justice, or lack thereof, of the death penalty. The answer to this last problem is today generally negative, on the basis of various positions taken, including those of the Magisterium, which it is not necessary to detail here. But one wonders if the problem is not actually deeper: what is the relation between a society that exercises its power of justice and the quality of the punishments inflicted, and how can this be determined in a manner that is not merely empirical? And there is a prior question to raise: what is the power of a society to exercise justice?

The third and last question is also truly fundamental: the absolute need for a stable juridical order that assures the just functioning of a society. A society, that is, where there is a sure guarantee, above and beyond changes, notably historical ones, and above all, beyond a "turn over" in personnel (as is now said). This need is evident in every area of human action, not only in the realm of political institutions. And the discussion could be extended and broadened, without too much delay, to the international realm as well. This world which is now globalized lacks a stable and universally valid juridical frame of reference which will ultimately make it just or, which will allow injustices to be identified, corrected and eventually condemned. The discussion thus returns to the first two problems already indicated. In fact, as is said in French, "*tout se tient*".

This is the overview in response to the kind invitation of Cardinal François-Xavier Nguyên Van Thuân, that I would present of the Pontifical Council for Justice and Peace, under the aspect of justice, insofar as this term is inseparable from the twofold title which identifies the Dicastery. While it is necessarily an incomplete description, it seems to me to give an idea of what the Pontifical Council has done, will do and could still do, to promote greater justice in this world and at this time. It will be for others to judge if this corresponds to the intentions of the Council Fathers or to those of the great Pontiff and Servant of God, Paul VI, the two promoters of the Dicastery for

Justice and Peace. The seed has, however, been sown. Its growth, flourishing and producing of fruit, is the work of those who came or who will come later. Our work was to plough the furrows and prepare the ground. This was by no means a small task. King of Justice and King of Peace, the Lord, like Melchizedek (cf. *Heb* 7, 2), will do the rest.

April 2002

THE DEFENCE AND PROMOTION
OF HUMAN RIGHTS

Archbishop ANDREA CORDERO LANZA
DI MONTEZEMOLO *

The theme of human rights did not explicitly appear in the initial mandate of the Pontifical Commission *Justitia et Pax*. The Motu Proprio *Catholicam Christi Ecclesiam* (6 January 1967) likewise did not refer to the theme when it entrusted two vast fields of work, those of development and peace, to the Commission.

Should this omission be considered a simple oversight, since human rights could be included in the question of peace? Could it rather be a sign that the theme was not yet "familiar" enough in the life of the Church, despite the attention given to it in the Encyclical *Pacem in Terris* (11 April 1963) and the recognition it had received in such documents of the Second Vatican Council as the Pastoral Constitution *Gaudium et Spes* and the Declaration *Dignitatis Humanae,* both of December 1965?

In the absence of the means for interpreting this omission, it is better simply to take note of it. At the same time, a similar lack also existed in the realm of public opinion where the theme never made the "front page", but remained confined to the reflections of specialists and the debates of international organisations. It did not even appear on university programs of study.

Actually, the Dicastery quickly perceived that human rights were of great importance and therefore merited careful examination in the light of the Council's teaching. As a result, the theme formed part of the agenda of the first Plenary Assemblies of the Commission, held in 1967 and in 1968.

In the same years, inter-governmental institutions took other initiatives, in particular through the United Nations' proclamation of 1968 as an International Year of Human Rights in order to mark the 20th anniversary of the Universal Declaration of Human Rights. The International Conference on Human Rights, which was held in Tehran in the same year, marked the starting point for a renewed commitment to the promotion and protection of human rights at the international level.

* Under-Secretary of the Pontifical Council for Justice and Peace from 1972 to 1974 and Secretary from 1974 to 1977.

On the part of the Church, on 1 January 1968, the first World Day of Peace was celebrated. It was an essentially pedagogical initiative launched by Paul VI to encourage the commitment to peace of all "true friends of peace" and that of the Church's faithful to prayer, through the annual proposal of a theme. The theme chosen for the second World Day of Peace, 1 January 1969, was "The promotion of human rights, the road to peace", a theme which gave clear proof of the attention that the Church was giving to human rights and which visibly accompanied the activity of the United Nations. This convergence was also brought out by Paul VI's historic visit to the United Nations Headquarters in New York (4 October 1965) and further confirmed by the Message he sent to the United Nations on the occasion of its 25th anniversary (4 October 1970).

In a similar context, the Commission tried to find a way to emphasise the Church's specific contribution to the cause of human rights, based on the principle that such rights were an expression of the fundamental dignity of every human person, created in the image of God and redeemed by the sacrifice of Jesus Christ.

The task of following and carefully examining questions concerning human rights was entrusted to a Study Committee for Peace, set up by the Dicastery in 1968. In so doing, it hoped that the close relationship between respect for human rights and the preservation of peace would be emphasised.

The Committee carried on its work from 1968 to 1975 under the leadership of the eminent Italian, Dr. Vittorino Veronese, the former Director General of UNESCO. The task of preparing the document *The Church and Human Rights* (published in 1975) was entrusted to this Committee. Intended to be a working tool for National Justice and Peace Commissions, it was the first text of the Holy See to examine carefully the attitude of the Church towards human rights. The document was well received and widely circulated. The numerous translations made by local Churches give witness to this.

This text also served as a concrete model, subsequently used for other publications, of the way in which the Dicastery could contribute to the promotion of human rights. It set out clearly the theological foundations on which the corresponding action of the local Churches must be based and sought to offer a type of *status quaestionis* of the problem, while not dealing with those questions of a technical nature that go beyond the competence of the Church.

Together with the "promotion" of human rights, the Commission soon ran up against the aspect of their "defence". This took the form of requests entreating its intervention on behalf of victims of violations of human rights.

It was not easy to find the most appropriate response to such requests, one that would give public witness to its solidarity with the victims while seeking more discrete ways of finding an efficacious solution.

Initially, after it had made certain public declarations, it became evident that the Commission risked being perceived from the outside primarily as a "tribunal" charged with condemning those responsible for the violations. This explained the increasing number of denunciations that the Dicastery received during the first years of its existence. Such a perception was not correct however, and actually distorted the identity of the Commission as an organism of the Church and therefore bound to act according to specifically ecclesial modes of procedure in contributing to the respect of human dignity.

In the Motu Proprio *Justitiam et Pacem* (10 December 1976), by which Paul VI established the Commission as a permanent Dicastery of the Holy See, human rights are mentioned at least four times: a clear sign that the experience gained and the specific importance of the theme were highly valued.

The major concern for the Church still remains that stated by the Council: "... it is always and everywhere legitimate for her to preach the faith with true freedom, to teach her social doctrine and to discharge her duty among men without hindrance. She also has the right to pass moral judgements, even in matters touching the political order, whenever fundamental human rights or the salvation of souls make such judgements necessary" (*Gaudium et Spes*, No. 76).

In brief, this means developing that dual pastoral activity of "proclaiming" and "denouncing" which had been recommended in the document previously mentioned: *The Church and Human Rights* (cf. Nos. 70-90).

The Church has received the mandate of announcing her message of salvation, love and hope to all peoples and in all situations. This message must be proclaimed even when the surrounding circumstances are in contradiction with it in that, whatever the situation may be, it is able to guide and support individuals in their journey towards the coming of the Kingdom, with an eschatological tension which is the keystone of the Christian commitment to the service of human rights.

Helping victims with all the means at her disposal, sharing in their sufferings through a supportive presence, rejecting the temptation to despair which leads people to violence: this is the difficult task proper to the Church in the field of human rights as she works in collaboration with the other Christian confessions, non-Christian religions, and all those of good will, according to the teaching of the Council.

On another level, the Church also does not tire of inspiring those structural transformations capable of acting on the profound causes of human rights violations, and of offering to Christians who assume their responsibilities in the political realm the help of a social doctrine that can strengthen their commitment.

If it is true that today there are some signs of fatigue concerning action for the promotion of human rights, it must nevertheless be acknowledged, in union with John Paul II, that such action remains a crucial aspect of the pastoral mission of the Church.

November 2002

THE RELATIONSHIPS
OF THE PONTIFICAL COUNCIL FOR JUSTICE AND PEACE WITH THE LOCAL CHURCHES

Bishop William F. Murphy*

From the beginning of its existence, the Pontifical Commission *Justitia et Pax* saw as part of its role an ongoing relationship with the local churches around the world. To a certain extent, this was a logical outgrowth of the Second Vatican Council which was the inspiration for Pope Paul VI's creation of the Pontifical Commission. Two movements intersect with each other during that particular period. One is the renewed emphasis on the local church and its role in the modern world. The second is the "justice and peace movement" itself, which gained much strength and vigor from the experience of the Second Vatican Council. In the aftermath of the Council, throughout the world but especially in Europe, there were outstanding laywomen and men who found a new dynamism in a relationship among themselves and with the Church that sought to promote the ideals and the values of social justice and world peace.

Msgr. Joseph Gremillion, the first Secretary of the Commission, was a personality who sought always to encourage as wide a variety of activities and initiatives as possible. To him it could rightly be said that one should "let a thousand flowers blossom". Therefore, in his role as Secretary, he encouraged as many new initiatives as he possibly could. That encouragement from Msgr. Gremillion was reinforced by members of the Pontifical Commission who themselves were leaders in the world of finance, labor and economics, with a special concern for developing countries in what had been recently termed by the United Nations "The First Decade of Development".

The particular work of the office can really be divided into two time periods. The first is from the formation of the Commission in 1967 by Pope Paul VI up to the publication of his Motu Proprio *Justitiam et Pacem* (1976). During the first period between 1967 and 1976, there was a phenomenal growth of national Justice and Peace Commissions. Ms. Marie-Ange Besson was one of the most active staff members of the Pontifical Commission

---

* Staff member of the Pontifical Council for Justice and Peace from 1974 to 1979 and Under-Secretary from 1979 to 1986.

encouraging the growth of national Justice and Peace Commissions. At one point in this early period, virtually every country in Latin America had a national Justice and Peace Commission. Western Europe, similarly, had Justice and Peace Commissions that were very active and brought together some of the most committed personalities in the field of social justice. In North America, both the United States and Canada formed national Justice and Peace Commissions in this period. This was less evident in Asia and in Africa although in certain countries, such as South Africa, that was certainly the case.

It is interesting to pause for a moment to see those Justice and Peace Commissions, both in themselves and in their relationship to the Pontifical Commission. First of all, none of them was directly dependent upon the Pontifical Commission. They were creations of the Conferences of Bishops in the countries where they existed. They saw the Pontifical Commission not as a parent body, but certainly as the point of reference to help them understand the kinds of activities that they themselves might make their own. There was, therefore, much correspondence between the office in Palazzo San Calisto and those national Commissions that sought help and advice, information and resources that otherwise they might not have. The national Commissions often reported to the Pontifical Commission the work that they were doing, and a close collaborative relationship, which was voluntary, was welcomed on both sides. Those organisms specifically involved in justice and peace initiatives locally were in direct contact with the Pontifical Commission, and a kind of mutual support, even a symbiosis, developed over time with some national Commissions and some leading personalities. There were some who even opined that this could be a new model for relations between the Holy See and the particular churches, a model that would bring to the particular country and to the world a sense of the credibility of the Church in the field of social justice, social action and social reform. In Europe, national Commissions were strong and led by strong personalities. These formed on their own a European Conference of Commissions. The Conference met annually as a group of Commissions concerned with European issues. In this, they followed the model of the Pontifical Commission's annual plenary meeting with its own members.

While the relationships were many and diverse between the Pontifical Commission and national Justice and Peace Commissions, that did not mean that in any way the Pontifical Commission gave an agenda to the national Commissions. On the contrary, the national Commissions that were brought into place by the local Conferences of Bishops were very much tailored to their own particular national issues. For example, in Chile, the national

25

Commission became very much involved in the issues of human rights at a time when the Chilean experience was oscillating between democracy under President Eduardo Frei and socialism under President Allende that ended ultimately with the military regime of General Pinochet. During those latter years the justice and peace work was carried on by the *Vicaría de Solidaridad*. In Brazil, the Justice and Peace Commission was very much concerned with issues of national security and later issues of land reform. In Great Britain, issues of human rights took a great deal of the attention of the national Commissions while other European Commissions became interested in the aftermath of colonialism in the newly independent countries of Asia and Africa.

The flourishing of these Commissions was, however, short-lived. There were several reasons for this. As one looks back, one could see a certain tendency among the members of the national Commissions to constitute themselves as a force or movement that interacted with the society often independently of the bishops themselves. Thus, once the Commission was given its mandate by the Bishops' Conference, it often happened that a national Commission became self-perpetuating, defining itself in terms of the issues of society. Recall that this was the time when the World Council of Churches had enshrined the slogan, "The world gives the church its agenda". Similarly, many of the leaders of the national Justice and Peace Commissions looked to the society and its challenges as the resource to which the national Commission was called to respond. This gave the Commissions an immediacy and a force in the particular society that was remarkable. At the same time, however, national Commissions became "actors" in the society that were at times seen as apart from the initiatives of the Conferences of Bishops themselves.

Given the changing political landscape in Latin America, some of the 23 national Justice and Peace Commissions that existed in 1971 slowly began either to disappear or to undergo change. The Commissions in Europe sometimes became more and more independent voices working rather on their own agenda. The Commissions in North America continued to operate within the context of the Conferences of Bishops even though they achieved a prominence that often made them the offices that took the initiative and set the agenda of church affairs in those countries.

The Motu Proprio *Justitiam et Pacem* of Paul VI, December 1976, delineated clearly and definitively the role of the Pontifical Commission for Justice and Peace. The essential points of that Motu Proprio were affirmed by Pope John Paul II in his Apostolic Constitution of 1988 on the reorganization of the Roman Curia, *Pastor Bonus*. Pope Paul VI made three major points. The first was that the Commission was a part of the Roman Curia and therefore was to be seen as a Dicastery, operating as the Dicasteries of the Roman Curia must act, *vis-à-vis* the Holy Father, the Secretariat of State and the other Dicasteries that make up the central organization of the Catholic Church. Second, it was to relate to the particular churches through their Episcopal Conferences themselves. Thus, the work of the Pontifical Commission was to be more closely linked to the bishops themselves. Thirdly, the substance of the work was to be the social doctrine of the Church. Social issues and topics were to be seen through the perspective of the social doctrine of the Church and not to be taken and considered apart from that social doctrine. It was clear that these three points so spelled out in the Motu Proprio of Paul VI would have an effect on the Pontifical Commission and its relationship to the national Justice and Peace Commissions.

In 1977, the then-Undersecretary of the Pontifical Commission, Reverend Roger Heckel, S.J., wrote a circular letter to all of the Episcopal Conferences. In that circular, he explained the implications of the Motu Proprio of Paul VI for National Commissions and Episcopal Conferences and their relationship to the Pontifical Commission. He pointed out that, in accordance with the wishes of the Sovereign Pontiff, the office of the Pontifical Commission would have regular and systematic contact with the Episcopal Conferences and, in agreement with the latter, give help and information to the locally created organisms in regard to the study of problems related to justice and peace. The concern of the Dicastery would always be one of service to the local churches as churches. He emphasized in this circular the centrality of the social doctrine of the Church. That centrality was to become the substance of the work of the Pontifical Commission because it is the substance of the Magisterium's proclamation of the truth about the human person in society. This social doctrine of the Church would scrutinize any ideologies or philosophies or theologies that might stand in contrast with or even in contradiction to the teaching of the Magisterium in the field of social justice and world peace. In the name of the office, Father Heckel then invited the Episcopal Conferences to deepen their direct relationships with the office and to make use of its resources in whatever ways would be helpful to the local churches.

In the subsequent quarter-century, the Pontifical Council (the official name was changed by the Apostolic Constitution *Pastor Bonus* of 1988), under the leadership of Cardinals Gantin, Etchegaray and Van Thuân, has deepened and expanded that basic commitment. The office staff has worked closely with Episcopal Conferences and their representatives in being a resource and an agent in helping develop the understanding of Catholic social doctrine in the local churches and seeing that applied to the particular challenges and social problems that Episcopal Conferences face in all the continents of the world. That work has benefited from the leadership of Pope John Paul II whose own contributions to Catholic social doctrine remain one of the hallmarks of his great pontificate. His encyclicals and discourses and addresses have enriched Catholic social teaching in a remarkable way. In turn, they have given to the Pontifical Council material that has allowed the members and the staff to deepen the work that they do and to expand the ways the Council is serving the local churches.

One example of this is the service that the Council provided to the church in the United States in the 1980s. That Episcopal Conference had proposed to develop a text on the challenge of peace in that decade, the last of the cold war. The then "Commission", particularly through the work of then-Father, now Cardinal Jan Schotte, C.I.C.M., Secretary of the Commission, developed a strong working relationship with the committee of the United States bishops drafting what became the pastoral letter on peace published by the U.S. bishops in 1983. The staff of the Commission was able to provide not only an analysis of many of the issues of peace in the 1980s, but to help the committee in the United States to apply the principles of Catholic social teaching to the many-faceted challenges that were posed at that time. Similarly, the Commission worked with the Conference of Bishops in Australia to analyze and review the actions of the national Justice and Peace Commission there. In that process, the Australian bishops were aided by the advice and counsel of the office of Justice and Peace at San Calisto in order to clarify what they wanted to have happen in terms of the local church's commitment to social justice in the context of Australian society.

One of the hallmarks of this new thrust were the frequent meetings of bishops who came to Rome for their *ad limina* visits. Annually, the presidency of the Council invited the bishops coming to the Holy See for that particular year to include a visit to San Calisto and to the offices of the Council as part of their *ad limina*. Large numbers of bishops through the past two decades have accepted this invitation and have had the opportunity to dialogue with the leadership and staff of the Pontifical Council on topics of mutual interest.

The Council has taken a particular interest from its very beginning in developing countries. Internally, the staff has for some time been organized so that specific staff members would follow the issues of a particular area of the world in addition to whatever specialized expertise that staff member might have. The Council as a whole has demonstrated a great commitment to the churches in Latin America, in Africa and in Asia.

28

In Latin America, the Pontifical Council has worked closely with CELAM, the joint Episcopal Conferences of Latin America and Mexico. They have together sponsored seminars and workshops. They have collaborated in special study weeks on the social doctrine of the Church.

Africa, too, has been an area of particular concern. While the issue of *apartheid* was a matter of special concern for some time, that was not the only topic that has been addressed by local churches with the help of the Pontifical Council. The Pontifical Council has developed close ties with SECAM, the Symposium of the Episcopal Conferences of Africa and Madagascar. The Council leadership, in addition, has visited Africa on many occasions and has taken part in a variety of seminars and symposia that have to do with development, with education and with strategies for economic viability and solidarity throughout the African continent.

In the years when Cardinal Gantin was President of the Commission, he made several trips to Asia. On these occasions, the Cardinal made it his prime objective to meet with leadership of the Episcopal Conferences and to enter into dialogue in various countries on issues of justice and peace. This work was expanded and developed much further under the leadership of Cardinals Etchegaray and Van Thuân. Indefatigable in their outreach to the Episcopal Conferences, Cardinals Etchegaray and Van Thuân engaged the Episcopal Conferences in all parts of the world to bring to them the resources and the insights of the Holy See, while at the same time offering them the strength and support of a brother as bishops struggled with the issues that were challenging their own societies.

Prominent among those who brought the Episcopal Conferences in deeper and deeper relationship with the Holy See on these issues was Archbishop Diarmuid Martin. As Secretary of the Pontifical Council, he was the spearhead of developing relationships with Africa at the beginning and then throughout the world. His understanding of the economic and financial issues of macro- and micro-economics contributed greatly to the ways that the Pontifical Council was able to offer advice and counsel with great expertise to bishops around the world.

With the establishment of the Council as a permanent part of the Roman Curia, the Holy Father had the opportunity to assure that the membership of the Council reflected the universality of the Church. In the last quarter-century, the membership of this Council very specifically has included leaders, both clerical and lay, from the local churches. Diocesan bishops, laywomen and laymen who are active in projects and initiatives in their local churches have served on five-year terms as members of the Pontifical Council. They have brought to the plenary sessions and to the ongoing work of the Council experience and insight that have enriched the universal social teaching of the Church with the practice of living the Gospel in the societies and cultures that make up the modern world. This has strengthened the links between the Holy See and the local churches and has enabled the leadership of the Council to understand more deeply some of the issues as they are lived out in various cultures. The Council, in turn, has been a great source of support to the Episcopal Conferences and to the local churches as they seek to be faithful to living the Gospel of Jesus Christ through the social doctrine of the Church.

Today, as in the past, the churches around the world look to the Holy See and to the Vicar of Christ, both to offer to them the tradition of the Church and its teaching and to give witness to them of the commitment of the Church to the apostolic mandate of Jesus Christ. The Council has responded to their needs and continues to do so in the third millennium. It has responded to the challenges of the debt issues, the various elements of international finance and the concerns that the Holy Father has for developing countries throughout the world. Prominent in the work of the Council in these recent years is the preparation of a Compendium of Social Doctrine which the Holy Father asked the Council to undertake in 1999 and which, under the careful guidance of the Secretary, Bishop Giampaolo Crepaldi, will be a contribution of singular importance to the local churches, and to Catholics and non Catholics alike in the years to come.

The Presidency, the members and the staff of the Pontifical Council have developed a privileged role, in accordance with the wishes of the Sovereign Pontiffs, to serve the local churches, as the Council serves the Holy Father and the offices of the Roman Curia, bringing to them the social doctrine of the Church as the way to analyze the societies in which we live and bring to those societies the insights of the Church based on the Gospel message of Jesus Christ and the lived experience of the Church's teaching Magisterium, a "true expert in humanity".

August 2002

ECUMENICAL COLLABORATION IN THE SOCIAL FIELD

Sr. Marjorie Keenan, RSHM*

I. Lessons Learned Along the Way

The ecumenical mission of the Pontifical Council for Justice and Peace [2] (PCJP) is actually implicit in the request of the Pastoral Constitution *Gaudium et Spes* that an organ of the universal Church be created to promote everywhere the justice and love of Christ for the poor.[3] Such a mission not only has no boundaries, its realization calls ultimately for the participation of all. In fulfilling this role, the Pontifical Council must therefore seek to co-operate actively with other Christian Churches in an attempt to promote "genuine universal solidarity and responsibility" among all peoples.[4] From its very foundation, the Pontifical Council for Justice and Peace has kept alive this desire for ecumenical collaboration.

Several challenges face the Pontifical Council for Justice and Peace in realizing this much-needed collaboration. Called to "promote justice and peace in the world, in the light of the Gospel and of the social teaching of the Church",[5] the Pontifical Council for Justice and Peace has neither on-going social programs nor projects as is the case for its principal ecumenical partner, the World Council of Churches (WCC). The size, structure, composition and practice of the two bodies are clearly different. Yet both share a common, if distinctive, responsibility: that of being at the service of the members of their respective Churches in view of the common good of all humanity.

A second challenge that the Pontifical Council for Justice and Peace faces in attempting to achieve common witness and action with the World Council of Churches is also of an ecclesial nature. The Pontifical Council is

---

* Member of the Pontifical Council for Justice and Peace from 1976 to 1986 and staff member from 1986 to 2000.

[2] The original title was Pontifical *Commission*. In 1988, Pope John Paul II changed its name to Pontifical *Council*. Throughout this text, the title *Council* or the initials PCJP will be used.

[3] Pastoral Constitution *Gaudium et Spes*, No. 90.

[4] *Ibid.*

[5] Apostolic Constitution *Pastor Bonus* (art. 142). Cf. Paul VI, *Populorum Progressio*, No. 5; Motu Proprio *Iustitiam et Pacem*, No. I-II.

called to give visible expression to the love of Christ for the poor. Crucial social problems generally arise in very concrete political and cultural contexts. It is generally the local church that assumes responsibility for the decisions taken precisely in the light of the universal principles of the Social Teaching of the Church. The laity also holds a major role in this task.[6] The World Council of Churches cannot, by its very nature, have a common theology or moral teaching in the social field. Similarly, it does not speak in a binding way for these Churches; its many well-developed programs are rather offered to the Churches.

A third difficulty in collaboration concerns common witness in the international field. The Holy See has internationally recognized juridical status and is an Observer State within the United Nations. In this capacity, it has the possibility of participating fully in international conferences. The World Council of Churches has the status of a non-governmental organization and participates in these same conferences on a different, if at times no less effective, level. Common stances are therefore not always possible within the international sphere.

These very concrete difficulties only heighten the challenge to the two bodies to seize every possibility to work together. At the same time, it is important not to overlook the consistent and growing ecumenical collaboration at the local level, often in very difficult and, at times, tragic situations of almost total lack of justice and of senseless violence. The PCJP and the WCC have had an important role in the encouraging of such collaboration. Since its foundation, the Pontifical Council for Justice and Peace has encouraged the establishment of national or local bodies within the particular church specifically dedicated to the promotion of justice and peace, while the World Council of Churches has offered significant help to its members, often National Councils of Churches, concerning the same situations.

II. An Experiment in Ecumenical Structures (1966-1988)

SODEPAX: the challenge of a joint ecumenical structure

The early days of the Pontifical Council for Justice and Peace reflect how seriously the ecumenical challenge was taken up. On 1 October 1967, the PCJP established a study group on peace and the international community with the specific intent of working in close relationship with the WCC. At the

---

[6] Cf. SECOND ECUMENICAL COUNCIL, Dogmatic Constitution *Lumen Gentium*, No. 36 and Decree *Apostolicam Actuositatem*, No. 7.

first meeting of the study group, a three-year program of ecumenical meetings was drawn up; collaboration was clearly meant to be ongoing.

The following year, however, it was decided to establish SODEPAX as a joint liaison body of the Catholic Church and the WCC for common action and witness in the social field. An independent office was set up in Geneva, and SODEPAX took over the program of the PCJP study committee on peace. Within a few short months, SODEPAX held a conference on *World Collaboration for Development* in Beirut, Lebanon. The evaluation of this highly successful meeting stated that it was easier to reach agreement on common interests than on a common theology of development. The Churches had, in fact, immediately recognized the importance of establishing solid theological foundations in their search for common witness as well as the difficulty of doing so.

Highly acclaimed SODEPAX meetings were also held in Montreal and Tokyo, and SODEPAX quickly became a symbol of ecumenical collaboration. Yet, as early as 1970, doubts began to arise. Should the work in the social field of the PCJP and the WCC always and uniquely be carried on through SODEPAX? Was their agenda necessarily always to be the same?

Despite this incipient questioning, the mandate of SODEPAX was renewed. It began to publish a review entitled *Church Alert* containing documents on social questions of interest to both bodies. It also developed a major program on sustainable development. Yet, by 1980, the parent bodies asked for a serious evaluation of the effectiveness of SODEPAX. Despite its high public profile, by mutual agreement this joint structure was dissolved in 1980. What were some of the reasons?

In the first place, SODEPAX was to have been a liaison body between the two parent bodies. It had, however, actually taken on a life of its own. Both parent bodies also questioned whether holding large conferences was the best means of collaboration. They were also increasingly aware of the importance of theological reflection if true ecclesial collaboration was to be achieved. In addition, many of the local churches were not responding to the SODEPAX program on sustainable development because the local Church Councils and Episcopal Conferences, above all in the West, were actively developing and implementing national programs concerning just and equitable development for all.

The Consultative Group on Social Thought and Action (1981-1988)

Since the parent bodies remained convinced that cooperation had to continue, they decided to set up a more modest and flexible body, *The Con-*

sultative Group on Social Thought and Action. This new body was to attempt to clarify certain *moral and ethical* issues in the social field and to promote *education and spiritual formation* for social commitment.

At its first meeting in September 1981, the Consultative Group decided to begin by exchanging information on specific topics. Peace, considered the great challenge of that time, was the chosen focus. A joint publication on disarmament containing statements of the parent bodies was realized in 1982.

The Consultative Group continued to meet regularly, but its reflections remained largely internal to the parent bodies. In 1985, it decided to establish an *ad hoc* group to study the highly important question of the theological foundations and significance of the social commitment of the Churches. The specific focus of the study was to clarify how the Churches could best continue to approach major social problems. Apartheid and religious liberty were signaled out for particular attention. This study was never completed.

The following year, agreement was reached on the need for the Churches to refuse racism on scriptural, theological and pastoral grounds. The Pontifical Council for Justice and Peace and the WCC Sub-Unit on Justice and Service were asked to continue a common reflection on apartheid as an expression of racism. At the 1987 meeting, a brief joint statement on the Christian Churches' common rejection of racism as a sin against the dignity of the human person and the unity of the human family was drawn up. The statement was never published.

In 1988, the mandate of the Consultative Group expired. No attempt was made to renew it or to establish another joint intermediary body.[7] However, collaboration began to take a new form that presented its own challenges: participation in the activities of the ecumenical partner. The timing was appropriate. The WCC General Assembly had recently decided to hold a major World Convocation on Justice, Peace and the Integrity of Creation in 1990. Would the Catholic Church agree to be a co-inviter? While the Catholic Church could not give an answer before knowing what was involved, it did accept to be a full participant in the preparatory process. Ecumenical collaboration was about to enter into a new phase.

---

[7] A collaborative body of the Catholic Church and the World Council of Churches still exists. The Joint Working Group was founded in 1964. Its mandate is not limited to the social field but covers the entire field of ecumenical relationships, primarily that of theological agreement. The Joint Working Group has closely followed the many difficult efforts of the two parent bodies to achieve common witness in the social field.

The closing of a first period of ecumenical collaboration

Throughout this period of challenging efforts to undertake joint programs or actions, the PCJP and the WCC continued to maintain direct relationships and regularly extended invitations to participate in each other's meetings. When Pope Paul VI had visited the World Council of Churches in 1973, he had encouraged the coordination of efforts and had added a new and important consideration: collaboration at such a high level presupposed the preparation of people on the local level for dialogue and collaboration. Independent efforts on the part of both parent bodies to help the churches on the local level were growing and already beginning to bear fruit in addressing concrete social problems.

In summary, the initial period of collaboration with the World Council of Churches was marked by a certain optimism coupled with a series of difficulties arising from the differences in nature of the bodies and in their approach to social questions. The will to continue to collaborate to the degree possible remained strong. It should be noted that the PCJP also had cordial direct relationships with other Churches within the Christian communion. At the time of apartheid, for example, relationships were particularly strong with the Lutheran World Federation and the Anglican Communion. Various Orthodox Churches also did not hesitate to express their common interest with the Catholic Church in questions of racism. These relations continue and take various forms.

III. The Challenges of Ecumenical Collaboration Today

A joint regional initiative

The Churches in Europe are well organised on a regional level. The Protestant and Orthodox Churches are united in a Council of European Churches, while the Catholic Episcopal Conferences meet in a Council of European Episcopal Conferences. Parallel but similar structures therefore existed. The two bodies decided to hold a joint meeting on justice, peace and the integrity of creation in May 1989 in Basel, Switzerland. The preparations for it were highly participative. A draft document was drawn up and sent to all the Churches and ecumenical groups concerned. Over six hundred replies were received. The document was entirely reformulated before being sent to the Churches a second time. At the meeting of almost seven hundred delegates, the final document was eventually adopted by 95.4% of those present and voting.

Five observer delegates from Vatican offices participated in this meeting, among whom representatives of the Pontifical Council for Justice and Peace. Its president, Cardinal Roger Etchegaray, delivered a major address in plenary. This was the first time that the Eastern European Churches were able to participate in such a gathering. It was startlingly clear how different their experience in the social field had been. While there was little follow-up to this meeting on the local level, a second such Pan-European meeting was held in Graz in 1997. Following it, a sentiment seemed to prevail that perhaps the time for such large gatherings with a vast agenda was over. Collaborative work on specific social concerns was now assuming growing importance.

The World Convocation on Justice, Peace and Integrity of Creation

In 1988, the Catholic Church had agreed to participate fully in the preparatory process for the WCC World Convocation on Justice, Peace and the Integrity of Creation. Two Catholics were appointed to work directly with the WCC in Geneva, while five others, coming from the Pontifical Council for Christian Unity, the Pontifical Council for Justice and Peace and the Congregation for the Doctrine of the Faith, were named to the Preparatory Committee.

Almost immediately several difficulties emerged concerning the basic moral concepts under-girding the Convocation, among which the meaning of covenanting when applied to creation itself and the role of the human person within creation. Another contentious question concerned the participants in the Convocation. Would the Convocation remain a meeting of representatives of the Churches or would participants from movements not recognized by their local church, or indeed rejected by them, also be invited? The Catholic Church, as well as other Churches, requested that the local churches name all the participants. This was not, however, to be the case.

With time, it became increasingly clear that the theological difficulties were growing. Many of the replies to the draft document sent to the Churches shared the concerns that had divided the Preparatory Committee. With great regret, the Catholic authorities finally made it known that they could not accept an invitation to be co-inviters to the Convention, nor could they send the requested delegation of fifty full participants. Twenty observer delegates would, however, be appointed. It was the only decision that could be taken in the light of lack of agreement on essential points.

During the Convocation, these same difficulties, divisions and, at times, serious disagreements arose despite the good will of all concerned, and the Convocation did not live up to expectations. Despite this, the very fact that the Convocation had been held focused the attention of the Churches across the world on very important social issues. It also brought care for the environment into the center of social concern. The phrase "the integrity of creation" now often stands alongside "justice and peace".

Modesty in collaborative efforts between the Catholic Church and the World Council of Churches now became the order of the day. One highly positive collaborative initiative was the appointment of a Catholic member to the Commission of the WCC Unit concerned with social questions, coupled with annual meetings of staff members of the two bodies. While the PCJP does not have ongoing programs, it invites the WCC to various meetings, and a staff member of the PCJP is a member of the WCC Group of Experts for the Decade to Overcome Violence.

Ecumenical collaboration in the field of the environment

Care for the environment is a social question with deep moral and theological implications of direct concern to the Churches. His All Holiness, Dimitrios I, the Ecumenical Patriarch of Constantinople, recognized the potential for organic collaboration in this field as early as 1991. He issued an invitation to all his brother Patriarchs and heads of the autocephalous Orthodox Churches across the world to a Pan-Orthodox Conference on Environmental Protection. An invitation was also extended to the other Churches to send an official observer. The Catholic Church was happy to reply positively and asked that a representative of PCJP attend.

This Conference marked the beginning of ongoing participation in the many environmental initiatives of His All Holiness Bartholomew I, successor to Dimitrios I. The Pontifical Council for Justice and Peace regularly participated in a series of summer seminars on the environment held on the island of Halki, off Istanbul. This initiative was soon paralleled by a series of high-level symposia focused on water as a key element in care for the environment. The four symposia already held have had a positive impact on the environmental awareness of the coastal countries of the Black Sea, the Danube River and the Adriatic. This fruitful collaboration over the years resulted in His All Holiness Bartholomew and His Holiness John Paul II signing a common Declaration on the Environment on 10 June 2002. Collaboration in the field of the environment is now ongoing.

Ecumenical collaboration within a secular context

The relative ease with which collaboration has become possible in the field of the environment points to other forms of indirect ecumenical collaboration that have borne fruit. When a serious social question has been identified, often by non-governmental organizations or governments, it is often possible for the Churches and other religious bodies concerned by the same problem to meet in a secular context and to re-reinforce one another's position without seeking to draw up a common document or to determine the details of a common public stance. This has been the case, among other, with the problem of the foreign debt of the poorer countries.

On the national or local level, coalitions now regularly meet on a series of social questions. The Churches often take part in them. Within this context, each Church is able to speak out of its own tradition and often informally sustain the positions with other Churches. The richness and strength of such exchanges comes precisely from their often complementary diversity.

Prayer for peace

On the eve of his death, Jesus left his followers the gift of peace. The search for this peace has been part of the mission of the Church across the centuries. Pope John Paul II reminded all of this so often ignored gift in 1986 when he called upon all believers to pray for peace. On 27 October 1886, the leadership of the Catholic, Orthodox and Protestant Churches, as well as that of the other world religions, gathered in Assisi to pray for peace. While the members of each tradition prayed according to their own religious beliefs, all were deeply united in praying for peace. Again on 24 January 2002, a similar Day of Prayer for Peace was held in Assisi. This and other similar prayer initiatives have created strong bonds among the various religions in the universal quest for peace.

A challenge that remains

In a world marked by instant communication and increasing globalization, the social problems of one part of the world quickly become those of all of humanity. Churches, religious bodies and, indeed, all persons of good will are now fully aware of the need to work together to assure the conditions of a peaceful world where the goods of the earth would be shared equitably and God's creation would not be destroyed for the benefit of the few. While differences in structure and scope may continue to make some forms of collaboration difficult, fruitful ecumenical collaboration is growing in unexpected ways and on many levels.

The Jubilee Year 2000 marked another decisive step forward in the realization among Christians of the intimate link between religious belief and the promotion of the human dignity of every member of the human family. This awareness remains perhaps the most forceful impetus for collaboration. The many ecumenical challenges in the social field are also an invitation to find new and creative ways of expressing the common profound conviction that all the followers of Christ are called to give clear witness to Christ's love for the poor. The Pontifical Council for Justice and Peace is now seeking to assure that all Catholics have an opportunity to know the Social Teaching of the Church and how to live in its spirit. This effort will certainly lead to new and perhaps unexpected ways of collaboration among Christians as they work to assure the dignity of each human person, of each people as well as the unity of the human family.

December 2002

PART II

A Deepening of Themes of Our Day

SOCIAL DEVELOPMENT
AND THE FIGHT AGAINST POVERTY

Professor Louis Sabourin[*]

Introduction

Approached for a long time from a strictly economic point of view, *development* has over the past forty years taken on many different dimensions, bringing together imperatives from the globalization of markets as well as various social and cultural aspects that are characteristic of countries, regions or localities, concerning objectives that are at the same time both worldwide and specific. Already at the beginning of the 1960s, authors such as Perroux[8] and Lebrer[9] were raising questions about the possibility of opting for a development that was more human and introduced the parameters for the debates on the following questions.

What place should *social factors* have in devising strategies for development? Up to what point do *social realities* depend on *economics*, and *economics* on *social realities*? By itself, can growth, based on increased production of goods and services, ensure the well-being of peoples? These are the questions that will be raised in the present analysis. The first part will show how the concept and practice of development has evolved during the last few decades, while the second part will examine the present situation, especially as far as the fight against poverty is concerned. The conclusion will then look briefly at the Church's position in this regard.

The Church, having remained for a long time a non-participant in the debates concerning economic development, has been showing increasing interest in the subject, above all from the 1960s, starting with the publication of John XXIII's Encyclical *Pacem in Terris*,[10] which dealt with peace in the world. The documents of the Second Vatican Council, especially *Gaudium*

---

[*] Director of International Group Study, Research and Formation, National School of Public Administration, University of Quebec; Former President of the Development Centre of the OECD; Member of the Pontifical Council for Justice and Peace from 1984 to 1996; from then on Member of the Pontifical Academy of Social Sciences.

[8] F. Perroux (1961), *De l'économie du XXe siècle*, Paris, Presses universitaires de France.

[9] L.-J. Lebrer (1961), *Dynamique concrète du développement*, Paris, Éditions Ouvrières.

[10] John XXIII (1963), Encyclical Letter *Pacem in Terris*.

et Spes in 1965,[11] focused their attention anew on the problems of the world. The establishment by Paul VI in 1967 of a new Dicastery, the Pontifical Commission for Justice and Peace, signaled a decisive turning point. The successive Presidents of the Council, Cardinals Roy, Gantin, Etchegaray and Nguyên Van Thuân, enlarged and gave greater depth to the area of the Church's reflections on matters of social development.[12]

Thus, the Church has contributed to creating spaces for reflection, especially concerning development and the right of each person to development. She has enriched the discussions on different social issues such as peace, justice and the protection of human rights. In fact, the Church has never ceased to promote ethics, respect and human dignity, brotherhood, indeed *universal solidarity*, making a set of moral and spiritual principles available to those making decisions and engaging in activity aimed at development.

I. From Economic Development to Social Development

The use of the term "development" dates back to well before its appearance in Article 22 of the Covenant of the *League of Nations*, which affirmed the existence of *degrees of development*. Scholars such as Marx and Leroy-Beaulieu used it in the 19th century. Lenin made use of it in 1899 in his work *The Development of Capitalism in Russia*.[13] Schumpeter had likewise drafted his *Theory of Economic Development* in 1911.[14]

Now, while a number of authors wrote about development at the beginning of the twentieth century, the concept, as it is used today, took on particular importance following the Second World War, especially with the

---

[11] SECOND VATICAN COUNCIL (1965), Pastoral Constitution on the Church in the Modern World *Gaudium et Spes*.

[12] Among other works, cf.: PONTIFICAL COMMISSION IUSTITIA ET PAX, *The True Dimensions of Development Today* (1982), texts presented by Monsignor W. Murphy; *International Economics: Interdependence and Dialogue* (1984); *At the Service of the Human Community: an Ethical Approach to the International Debt Question* (1986); and PONTIFICAL COUNCIL FOR JUSTICE AND PEACE, *The Right to Development, Conciliar and Pontifical Texts (1960-1990)* (1991), presented by G. Filibeck; *Une terre pour tous les hommes. La destination universelle des biens* (1992), Centurion; *World Development and Economic Institutions* (1994); *The Modern Development of Financial Activities in the Light of the Ethical Demands of Christianity* (1994), by A. de Salins and F. Villeroy de Galhau.

[13] V. LENIN (1974), *Théorie du développement économique*, Paris, Éditions Sociales.

[14] J. A. SCHUMPETER (1967), *Theory of Economic Development, an Inquiry into Profits, Capital, Credit, Interest and Business Cycle*, New York, Oxford University Press.

arrival of new international actors on the scene.[15] At that time, the *International Bank for Reconstruction and Development* and the *International Monetary Fund* came into being with the signing of the *Bretton Woods Accords* in 1944. The *United Nations Organization* is likewise established in 1945, replacing the defunct League of Nations. Shortly after its foundation, the UN adopts two resolutions entitled *Economic Development of Insufficiently Developed Nations* and *Assistance Looking to Economic Development*. These resolutions affirm the importance of the process of development.

For its part, the United States sets the foundations for the *Marshall Plan* in 1947. In his *State of the Union Address*[16] of 1949, President Truman reiterates his country's desire to support the UN, to assist reconstruction in Europe and to create a common organization for defence (NATO) to counteract Stalin's ambitions. In the fourth point of his address, he likewise announces the possibility of lending *technical assistance* to disadvantaged nations; up to that time such assistance had been granted only to certain countries of Latin America. The text makes reference elsewhere to the notion of *under-development*, using the adjective "under-developed", making it understood that development was a possible means for reducing the gap between certain countries.

Thus, in November 1949 the General Assembly of the United Nations approves the creation of the *Expanded Programme of Technical Assistance* which provides for the sending of experts, the formation of teams and the granting of subsidies to nationals of developing countries. The World Bank broadens its activity and in 1956 creates the *International Financial Society* to support private investments. Moreover, in 1960 it sets up the *International Development Association*, entrusted with the task of making available to poor countries loans at conditions that are more favourable than those offered by the market. Similarly, after a preliminary attempt, the *United Nations Special Fund for Economic Development* is created. In 1965 this Fund was merged with the Expanded Programme of Technical Assistance, and the *United Nations Development Programme* was born.

It is in this context of bubbling international activity that the *Bandoeng Conference* in Indonesia takes place in 1955. This meeting marks the unofficial beginning of the *non-aligned movement* and the start of collective de-

---

[15] L. SABOURIN (1996), "Inégalités et développement", in *The Study of Tensions Between Human Equality and Social Inequalities from the Perspectives of Various Social Sciences*, Proceedings of the First General Assembly of the Pontifical Academy of Social Sciences, Vatican City, pp. 141-163.

[16] H. S. TRUMAN (1949), *Public Papers of the President of the United States*, 5, United States Government Printing Office.

mands made by the *Third World*. The participating States call in a special way for the decolonization of the South and emphasize the need for development by way of greater integration into the world economy. Several countries, especially from Africa, achieve independence at the end of the 1950s and the beginning of the 1960s. In 1962, the 1960s are proclaimed the *United Nations Decade for Development*.

It is at this time that development becomes closely connected to the level of economic growth of States. Expounded by Domar [17] in the 1950s, the *theory of growth* counts on the increase in national productions, principally by means of international aid in capital, technical assistance and private foreign investment. The Gross National Product is then the standard *par excellence*, if not the only measure used, for evaluating a country's progress. It is likewise at this moment that Walt W. Rostow comes up with his *evolutionist theory*. In his manifesto on the stages of economic growth, published in 1960, [18] Rostow describes development as a process made up of five linear stages, modeled after the evolution of Western countries: the *traditional society*, followed by the establishment of the *preliminary conditions* for "taking off", the "*take-off*" itself, *progress towards maturity* and *mass consumption*.

Supported by the majority of industrialized countries, this *theory of modernization* designates *urbanization, industrialization* and the *market economy* as the principal driving forces of development. Nonetheless, it is the object of strong opposition on the part of representatives of certain countries, especially in Africa and Latin America. Among other theories, these countries lean towards the *theory of dependence* to explain the inequalities between the nations of the North and those of the South, and they consider under-development as the result of an unfavourable international environment on the level of technology, commerce and finances.

The 1970s appear to hold better prospects for the countries of the South. The Third World nations are determined to make their points of view heard. The *non-aligned movement*, born in Belgrade in 1961, grows larger. The *United Nations Conference for Trade and Development*, founded in 1964, becomes a privileged place for the *Group of 77* to express themselves. In 1967 this latter group adopts the *Algiers Charter*, which brings together the various demands of the countries of the South with regard to their industrialized neighbours.

[17] E. D. DOMAR (1957), *Essays in the Theory of Economic Growth*, New York, Oxford University Press.
[18] W. W. ROSTOW (1960), *The Stages of Economic Growth. A Non-Communist Manifesto*, Cambridge, Cambridge University Press.

In 1970 the General Assembly of the United Nations proclaims the second *Decade for Development*, against the background of a strategy aimed at a more global and integrated action. Likewise, in 1974, at the demand of the non-aligned countries, it convokes an extraordinary session to study the problems related to primary materials and development. It is thus that the *Declaration on the Establishment of a New International Economic Order (NIEO)*, accompanied by a programme of action, and the *Charter of Economic Rights and Duties of States* take form. By means of these two resolutions, the New International Economic Order provides for a new sharing of the benefits of growth. A source of motivation from its inception, the New International Economic Order will never move beyond being a proposed project, for in 1981, at the *Cancun Conference*, the newly elected President Reagan, with the support of Mrs. Thatcher, has it terminated.

Moreover, the 1970s bring the rise of the *fundamental needs approach*. The idea was launched in 1972 by Robert McNamara, then President of the World Bank. In light of the difficulties facing certain countries, President McNamara stresses the need to increase the quality of life for the poorest peoples. Among other things, he counts on an increase of public aid to developing countries and invites governments to take into account the *most essential human needs*, such as nutrition, housing, health, education and employment. The *fundamental needs approach* is taken up afterwards in many different settings, especially by the *International Labour Organization*, at the *World Conference on Employment* in 1976. It receives considerable support, rallying international institutions working for development and numerous non-governmental organizations, which become ever more present in the world of international development.

At the same time, the *Dag Hammerskjöld Report*, a review document entitled *What Now?*, published in 1975,[19] adds new elements. Particularly, it considers development as a *global phenomenon* that goes well beyond economic issues, being an area of concern both for under-developed countries and developed countries. It also proposes a development based on the *satisfaction of the essential needs* of poor societies, the *principle of collective autonomy*, the *changing of structures* — among others, the structures of the United Nations and those that guide a country's internal policies — as well as *respect for ecological limits*. More and more, those who support a more qualitative approach speak up and denounce the overly quantitative and linear character of traditional theories of economic development.

[19] *What Now?*, The 1975 Dag Hammerskjöld Report on Development and International Cooperation, published in the Journal of the Hammerskjöld Foundation, *Development Dialogue*, ½, 1975.

For their part, the Western countries decide to meet with 19 countries from the South. This meeting takes place in Paris between February 1976 and November 1977 within the framework of the Conference on International Economic Cooperation, known also as the *North-South Dialogue*, and the principal point of discussion is energy, especially the allotment of oil, primary materials, trade, development and monetary and financial problems. Finally, the *Rio Report*,[20] published by the Club of Rome in 1976, recommends the liberalization of the movement and exchange of capital while also focusing attention on poor countries; the issue once again is that of reducing inequalities.

Not all the initiatives advocating a more human development, however, helped to spruce up the dinner tables of those who are poorest. Already in 1979, the *United Nations Research Institute for Social Development* notes a gap between real economic and social evolution of countries and the goals of development set by the *Charter of the United Nations*, the *Universal Declaration of Human Rights*, the *International Covenant on Economic, Social and Cultural Rights* and the *International Covenant on Civil and Political Rights*.[21]

It is therefore against this not-so-comforting background, without forgetting the growing debt and the economic recession of the 1980s, that the measures for *structural adjustment* are born. Proposed by the International Monetary Fund, these measures are intended to address the balance of payments by mitigating a certain number of qualifiable inequalities, inequalities due to a fall in world prices, the small volume of foreign investments, an excess of importations, the burden of debt repayment, the setting up of costly infrastructures, corruption, fiscal fraud, etc. Let us also stress, among the numerous causes, the eagerness of industrialized countries to recycle petro-dollars from 1975 on, combined with a rise in interest rates. This last factor also explains in large part the *Mexican crisis* of 1982. At the time, Mexico's foreign debt totaled 80 billion dollars. Moreover, the policies of structural adjustment will be largely disputed because of their negative effects on societies, occasioned by cuts in public services, in education, health, food, transportation and other areas directly affecting the poorest populations.

Ecology takes on a similar sense of importance during the 1980s with the introduction of the concept of *sustainable development*. The report *Our Com-*

[20] J. Ettinger (director), J. Tinbergen (coordinator) and A. J. Dolam (editor) (1976), *Reshaping the International Order, A Report to the Club of Rome*, New York, E. P. Dutton & Co.
[21] United Nations Research Institute for Social Development (1979), *Social Development and the International Strategy for Development*, Geneva.

mon Future,[22] published in 1988 by the *World Commission on Environment and Development,* assembles a complete inventory of environmental problems, from deforestation to the allotment of water, passing through soil deterioration, the hot-house effect, deterioration of the ozone layer, urbanization and other problems. The concept of *sustainable development,* based on satisfying human needs and preserving the ecosystem as much as possible so that future generations are not prevented from satisfying their needs, can be traced back to this report. The Commission's recommendations will lead in 1992 to the *Summit of the Earth* at Rio de Janeiro. The *Rio Declaration,* the *Convention on Climatic Change,* the *Convention on Biodiversity,* the *Declaration on Forests, Agenda 21* and the *Charter of the Earth* will all follow from this great gathering, bringing together more than 30,000 people.

Lastly, the 1990s are also the years of the *South Commission.*[23] Composed of commissaries and experts coming from a good part of the southern hemisphere and under the presidency of the former Tanzanian President Julius K. Nyerere, the Commission explores a certain number of problems: population growth, industrialization, international trade, South-South cooperation, international aid, fundamental needs, environment, etc. The Commission's conclusions however are a source of great disappointments, presenting anew several overly used reports without so much as suggesting any possible solutions or changes.

The relaunching of discussions on development goes back rather to the United Nations Development Programme, thanks to a completely new idea, that of *human development.* One of the first appearances of this expression is found in the *1990 World Report on Human Development.*[24] The experts sent by the United Nations Development Programme drafted first of all a new *index of human development,* which combines revenue, life expectancy and level of education. Suddenly, growth and the measurement of growth, which is what the gross national product is supposed to be, no longer suffice for evaluating the quality of individual lives. A second innovation, which is presented in 1991, is connected with the evaluation of the allocation of available funds. The United Nations Development Programme suggests a new formula for the distribution of aid, one that is more firmly based on

[22] WORLD COMMISSION ON ENVIRONMENT AND DEVELOPMENT (1987), *Our Common Future,* Oxford, Oxford University Press.

[23] See: SOUTH COMMISSION (1990), *Défis au sud* (Challenges for the South), Paris, Economica.

[24] UNITED NATIONS DEVELOPMENT PROGRAMME (1991), *World Report on Human Development,* Paris, Economica.

the definition of social priorities. It seeks to ascertain whether the funds allocated really improve the living conditions of the poor.

As far as the definition of the concept of *human development* is concerned, it refers to the *increasing of possibilities* for every person and includes many concepts, among which *political, economic and social freedom, creativity, productivity, self-respect* and *participation in the life of the community*. *Human development*, like all the previously mentioned concepts, is characterized moreover by a marked gap between the intentions underlying it and what is experienced in reality, which is a clear instance of the inequalities between rich countries and poor countries, gaps which not only continue in our day but which seem to grow wider after more than 50 years of research and sustained action on behalf of development. This does not overlook the fact that the ambitions of certain people have often clashed with those of others, under the cover of official or unofficial policies, which themselves give rise to a series of often contradictory interpretations of the real positions of various groups of people, indeed of the true intentions of each person.

II. Current Trends and the Fight Against Poverty

But where are we today with regard to development, more specifically, with regard to *social development*, and what can we expect over the course of the next few years? Far from being simple, this question could be the subject of a voluminous document all by itself. It is nonetheless possible to identify some key ideas. First of all, often placed in opposition to economic development, social development claims to be more *global*, including a whole series of factors, for example, education, employment, health, family, integration of the marginalized, without neglecting several factors of an economic order, such as availability of capital, investment, the degree of commercial initiatives, etc. Moreover, a number of those involved in this field are in agreement in saying that true social development — more equitable, inclusive and sustainable — cannot be brought about apart from economic development. The majority is also of the opinion that it is necessary to set up credible institutions — both local and regional, national and international — that keep watch over a greater participation of each and every person in a process of development that involves a more extensive cooperation between the State and civil society both at the national level and on a worldwide scale.

Regarding a model based principally on the economic growth of States, development has known different trains of thought and has gone through various stages during the last forty years. There has been gradually introduced the need to take into account a series of aspects for evaluating the foundedness and, above all, the effectiveness of strategies preferred by those working in the area of development throughout the world. Thus, other ideas have been grafted onto traditional models of development, even very recently with the appearance of new concepts, whether that of the *popular economy*, of the *economy of solidarity*, of the *plural economy*, of the *social economy*, or still yet of *local* or *worldwide governance*. These different approaches seek essentially to achieve a better integration of the economy into social realities and to tap the potentials of countries, regions or social communities. More than dealing with questions of subsistence, these approaches advocate the mobilization of each person's efforts in productive and creative activity in order to support, at their very foundations, the systems of local exchanges, in their social pertinence, so as to improve the conditions of life.

There are those as well who refer to this type of model as *first development* since it encourages the growth of local communities and the formation of an economic fabric among neighbours, in order later to integrate them into the overall development of the country. There are others who attribute to it the form of a *tripolar economy*: the first pole being reserved to the market economy, in correspondence to the private sector; the second pole referring to the non-market economy, or the public sector; the third pole designating the non-monetary economy, whether activities of autonomous production, volunteer activity, bartering and other types of activity. Of course, the first of these poles claims to be the most efficient, but it is a source of disparities. The second permits a greater equality but it runs into problems with bureaucratic limits. The desired goal, then, is to find an equilibrium between the three sectors in order to strengthen the social fabric by means of better sustained and better organized activity directly oriented to the greater well-being of the peoples concerned, and all this without setting aside the responsibilities of the State and the market forces that are necessary for ensuring sustainable development.

The *International Conference on the Social Economy of North and South*, held in Ostende in 1997,[25] and the *Lima International Conference*[26] of the same year are among the number of international meetings that have contributed to the promotion of this approach and have facilitated the debate regarding its viability. Overall, those involved are in agreement in recognizing that the small projects worked out at the level of civil society can never be sufficient. On the other hand, the discussions bring out the usefulness of

---

[25] See: J. DEFOURNY, P. DEVELTERE and B. FONTENEAU (1999), *L'économie sociale au Nord et au Sud*, Paris, De Boeck University.

[26] See: H. ORTIZ ROCA and I. MUNOZ (1998), *Simposio internacional Globalización de la Solidaridad, Un reto para todos*, Lima, Peru, GES/CEP.

these participatory initiatives in fostering the involvement of all levels of a society, including the poorest. Other gatherings have also enriched the debate concerning international development, among others the *Summit on Social Development*, which took place in Copenhagen in 1995,[27] and from which emerged a programme of action aiming principally at the creation of a favourable environment for social development, for the eradication of poverty and for greater access to employment and social integration.

However, it is quite legitimate to wonder about the viability of this new understanding of development in the fight against poverty. Does an economy — whether social, solidarity-based or plural — offer realistic long-term prospects? We must guard against too much enthusiasm, against moving too quickly. The idea is interesting and may prove to be effective in certain communities that have a minimum of resources. All the same, it has to be accompanied by the goodwill of local administrators as well as by a minimum of expertise and financial aid on the part of private investors or organizations and foreign governments, without forgetting the need for the populations involved to be able to take the situation in hand for themselves.

Nor does this take into account the fact that the various approaches put forth in the last few decades have not succeeded in attaining the goals pursued by the international community, especially regarding the fight against poverty. Certainly, development has enabled a number of countries to increase their national production considerably and, in specific cases, to raise the people's overall standard of living, particularly in South-East Asia. Nonetheless, in many States, regions, cities and local communities the number of those in poverty has increased rather than diminished.

Even the World Bank's strategy against poverty,[28] begun in 1990 and based on the productive use of manual labour, on the offering of social services in the areas of health, education, family planning and nutrition, and on the setting up of transfer programmes and security networks in certain targeted regions, has been the source of many disappointments. The Bank concludes that *its strategy remains relevant*, although it must be sustained by a *more holistic approach*. Regarding the progress achieved in the last decade, it remains modest despite an increase in international loans.

---

[27] See: UNITED NATIONS (1996), *Report of the World Summit for Social Development: Copenhagen 6-12 March 1995*, New York, and United Nations (1995), *The Copenhagen Declaration and Programme of Action / World Summit for Social Development*, New York.
  [28] WORLD BANK (2000), *Poverty Reduction in the 1990s. An Evaluation of Strategy and Performance*, Washington, D.C.

The World Bank has sought to adjust its actions. In its *World Development Report 2000/2001*,[29] it proposes a strategy that acts on three fronts: the development of *material opportunities*, in terms of employment, credit access, access to schools and health care, construction of roads and electrical networks, availability of drinking water, etc.; the *integration of the poor*, especially their participation in political, social and institutional processes, as well as the consideration of their needs in public administration; and lastly, *material security*, in order to assist societies to improve their management of financial, ecological and other risks, and to encourage investment in human capital.

To succeed in this, the Bank counts on different types of action, some based on economic growth, such as recourse to private investment endowments, the expansion of international markets and the setting up of infrastructures. Other actions are principally oriented to institutional reforms, like the decentralization of activities and the promotion of community-based initiatives, enhancing associative capital, creating local and regional networks, dismantling social barriers, improving the juridical context and initiating a debate on marginalization. Lastly, a third series of actions rest on the establishment of national programmes and systems for improving the management of social, civil and climatic risks and those connected with certain health problems, such as AIDS.

In addition to the World Bank, the United Nations too has fine-tuned its approach. The UN aims for example at *agriculture*, specifically at increasing productivity and at modernization of equipment, at the development of *human capital*, by way of education, formation and research, in order to increase significantly the technological abilities of workers, and at *institutional reinforcement*, in order to improve the functioning of the market, increase regional cooperation and encourage relations between the public and private sectors, and all this for the purpose of evading the *snare of poverty*.[30]

Nor does this neglect the various initiatives led by other international, national, civil or religious organizations or associated agencies in matters of social and economic development. It remains to be seen whether the strategies heretofore put forth will permit the attainment of the worldwide goals for development set for 2015. The big international players hope thus *to reduce by half the number of people living in extreme poverty, to provide primary education for all children, to make progress towards the equality of*

---

[29] WORLD BANK (2001), *World Development Report 2000/2001, Attacking Poverty*, New York, Oxford University Press.

[30] See: UNITED NATIONS (2000), *World Economic and Social Survey 2000, Trends and Policies in the World Economy*, Department of Economic and Social Affairs, New York.

the sexes and the independence of women, to reduce by two-thirds the rate of infant and juvenile mortality, to reduce by three-fourths the rate of mortality in child-birth, to place genetic health services within reach of all who need it and *to apply national strategies based on sustainable development.*[31]

In this regard, the numbers published by the World Bank are very significant.[32] Between 1987 and 1998, the proportion of people in developing countries earning less than a dollar per day fell from 28% to 24%. Nonetheless, when the increase in population is taken into account, it seems that the actual number of poor people has remained the same. Likewise, if the statistics have proven to be positive in Eastern Asia and in the Middle East and North Africa, they have decidedly grown worse in Southern Asia, in Europe and Central Asia, and in Sub-Saharan Africa. In these regions, the number of poor people has increased respectively from 474 to 522 million, from 1.1 to 24 million, and from 217 to 219 million. The World Bank has also recorded an increase of 20% in Latin America and the Caribbean.

As far as social indicators are concerned, these seem to have improved over the last 30 years. The World Bank cites the example of the infant mortality rate, falling from 107 out of every 1000 births in 1970 to 59 in 1998. This does not exclude the fact that in certain regions of Africa the infant mortality rate has, on the contrary, increased, especially in Sub-Saharan Africa where AIDS is causing mortality to rise. Similar regional disparities can be seen in the area of education. For example, if the overall level of children going to school has increased in Southern Asia, in Sub-Saharan Africa it remains unchanged.

To this we can add numerous disparities between countries and within the same country. The ratio between richer countries and poorer countries has reportedly changed from 35 to 1 in 1950, to 44 to 1 in 1973, and to 72 to 1 in 1992, according to the data of the Organization for Economic Cooperation and Development.[33] Today it would be valued at approximately 74 to 1. It was 3 to 1 in 1820. The richer countries, which account for one-fifth of the world population, would also have a per capita income that is 74 times greater than that in poorer countries. Moreover, all indications are that the gap between the member countries of the Organization for Economic Cooperation and Development and poorer countries threatens to increase even more through 2020.

[31] WORLD BANK (2001), *World Development Report 2000/2001, Attacking Poverty*, New York, Oxford University Press.

[32] *Ibid.*

[33] Data drawn from: ORGANIZATION FOR ECONOMIC COOPERATION AND DEVELOPMENT (2001), *La société créative du XXIe siècle, études prospectives*, Paris.

The international community, then, is facing some serious challenges, not only in the area of poverty but also in matters of redistribution of wealth, access to education and health care, justice and social protection, democracy, security, the environment, the functioning of institutions, making States more responsible, worldwide support and still others. This calls for the establishment of new governing structures [34] that require more closely monitored cooperation between the different sectors involved, public and private, both at the national and worldwide levels.

Conclusion

Towards a New Social Development: Challenges for the Church

Development has become a concern of every country, the more developed as well as the less developed. The repercussions of being excluded are felt even in the most prosperous societies. In like manner, environmental problems affect every territory regardless of its gross national product, prompting governments to adopt common measures. Another problem is found in the population deficit seen in many industrialized nations. There are vast migrations of peoples in many different places, which raises numerous challenges in matters of integration and cultural diversity, without forgetting the lot of clandestine immigrants and of refugees knocking at the borders of rich countries. To this must also be added the globalization of commerce which makes societies ever more interdependent among themselves.

Will the emergence of new stakes and the drafting of new strategies in the area of *social development* encourage the establishment of a world order after the events of 11 September 2001? It is still too early to tell. It is all the more possible to affirm that the world has entered a period of transition, which has prompted some serious questioning, especially concerning sensible means for guaranteeing the security and prosperity of peoples. For any given period of change, it is possible to envision divergences between the different parties involved, as much on ideological and geostrategic grounds as on the political, economic and social level. Now, the principal characteristic of our modern world is that we live in a "finite world" in which all peoples are becoming more and more interdependent. We are all responsible for finding common solutions to the problems we have in common. Everyone is involved.

[34] L. SABOURIN (2000), *La gouvernance globale, astuce passagère ou prémices d'un modèle de gestion en vue de mieux maîtriser la mondialisation?*, Treviso, International Institute Jacques Maritain.

The Church has a unique role to play in the changes taking place internationally. By means of her reflections and her social doctrine she can contribute to the humanization of international economic relations and foster a greater solidarity on the national level and on an international scale, encouraging all the while a development more firmly based on respect and equity among human beings. She can not only enlighten individual and collective consciences but also plant seeds of hope by promoting — that is, devising — new modes of behaviour, in respect for her religious, spiritual, moral and ethical functions.

Do not the preferential option for the poor and the importance of solidarity appear among the number of priorities presented by Pope John Paul II in his Encyclical *Sollicitudo Rei Socialis* of 1987? [35] In this regard, the Pontifical Council for Justice and Peace will always have new challenges to meet, especially in putting the Church's social doctrine to good use in the field of social development and in the fight against poverty. [36]

May 2002

Selected Bibliography

Arès, Richard (1977), *L'Église dans le monde d'aujourd'hui,* Présentation pédagogique de la Constitution pastorale "Gaudium et Spes", Montréal, Les Éditions Bellarmin.

Calvez, Jean-Yves (1989), *L'économie, l'homme, la société*, Paris, Desclée de Brouwer.

Calvez, Jean-Yves (1994), *L'Église devant le libéralisme économique, Petite encyclopédie moderne du christianisme*, Paris, Desclée de Brouwer.

Carrier, Hervé, S.J. (1990), *The Social Doctrine of the Church Revisited, A Guide for Study*, Document of the Pontifical Council for Justice and Peace, Vatican City.

Commission Sud (1990), *Défis au Sud*, Paris, Economica.

Defourny, Jacques, Develtere, Patrick and Fonteneau, Bénédicte (ed.), with the collaboration of Sophie Adam (1999), *L'économie sociale au Nord et au Sud*, Paris, De Boeck University.

De Salins, Antoine and Villeroy De Galhau, François (1994), *The modern development of financial activities in the light of the ethical demands of Christianity*, Document of the Pontifical Council for Justice and Peace, Vatican City, Libreria Editrice Vaticana.

[35] John Paul II (1988), *Sollicitudo Rei Socialis*, Encyclical Letter published on the occasion of the 20th anniversary of the Encyclical *Populorum Progressio*, Vatican City.

[36] I wish to thank Miss Annie Lirette, my research assistant, for her help in preparing this study.

Domar, Evsey David (1957), *Essays in the Theory of Economic Growth*, New York, Oxford University Press.

Ettinger, Jan van (dir.), Tinbergen, Jan (coord.) and Dolam, Antony J. (ed.) (1976), *Reshaping the International Order, A Report to the Club of Rome*, New York, E.P. Dutton & Co.

Favreau, Louis (resp.) (2000), "Économie sociale, coopération Nord-Sud et développement", *Économie et solidarité – Revue du Ciriec-Canada*, Presses de l'Université du Québec, vol. 31, no. 2.

Filibeck, Giorgio (comp.) (1991), *The right to development, Conciliar and pontifical texts (1960-1990)*, Document of the Pontifical Council for Justice and Peace, Vatican City.

John XXIII (1961), Encyclical Letter *Mater et Magistra*, Vatican City.

John XXIII (1963), Encyclical Letter *Pacem in Terris*, Vatican City.

John Paul II (1988), Encyclical Letter *Sollicitudo Rei Socialis*, Vatican City.

John Paul II (1991), Encyclical Letter *Centesimus Annus*, Vatican City.

Lebret, Louis-Joseph (1961), *Dynamique concrète du développement*, Paris, Éditions ouvrières.

Lénine, Vladimir Il'ich (1974), *Théorie du développement économique*, Paris, Éditions sociales.

Leo XIII (1891), Encyclical Letter *Rerum Novarum*, Vatican City.

OECD - Organization for Economic Cooperation and Development (1996), *Réconcilier l'économique et le social, Vers une économie plurielle*, Paris.

OECD - Organization for Economic Cooperation and Development (2001), *La société créative du XXIe siècle, Études prospectives*, Paris.

Ortiz Roca, Humberto and Muñoz, Ismael (1998), *Simposio Internacional Globalización de la Solidaridad, Un reto para todos*, Lima Perù, GES/CEP.

Papini, Roberto et al. (1989), *Etica ed economia I*, Genova, Marietti.

Paternot, Jacques and Veraldi, Gabriel (1989), *Dieu est-il contre l'économie?*, Lettre à Jean-Paul II, Paris, Éditions de Fallois.

Paul VI (1967), Encyclical Letter *Populorum Progressio*, Vatican City.

Perroux, François (1961), *De l'économie du XXe siècle*, Paris, Presses universitaires de France.

Pius XI (1931), Encyclical Letter *Quadragesimo Anno*, Vatican City.

PNUD (1991), *Rapport mondial sur le développement humain*, Paris, Economica.

Pontifical Commission "Iustitia et Pax" (1982), *The True Dimensions of Development Today*, Texts presented by Msgr. W. Murphy, Vatican City.

Pontifical Commission "Iustitia et Pax" (1984), *International Economics: Interdependence and Dialogue*, Contributions of the Holy See on the occasion of UNCTAD VI, Vatican City.

Pontifical Commission "Iustitia et Pax" (1986), *At the service of the human community: an ethical approach to the international debt question*, Vatican City.

Pontifical Council for Justice and Peace (1992), *Une terre pour tous les hommes, La destination universelle des biens*, Colloque international "Justice et Paix", 13-15 mai 1991, Paris, Centurion.

Pontifical Council for Justice and Peace (1994), *World Development and Economic Institutions*, Vatican City.

PUEL, HUGUES (1989), *L'économie au défi de l'éthique – essai d'éthique économique*, Paris, Cujas/Cerf.

RICHARD, JEAN and O'NEIL, LOUIS (dir.) (1993), *La question sociale hier et aujourd'hui*, Colloque du centenaire de *Rerum Novarum*, 12-17 mai 1991, Sainte-Foy, Presse de l'Université Laval.

RIST, GILBERT (1996), *Le Développement, Histoire d'une croyance occidentale*, France, Presses de la Fondation nationale des sciences politiques.

ROSTOW, WALT W. (1960), *The Stages of Economic Growth. A Non-communist Manifesto*, Cambridge, Cambridge University Press.

ROUSTANG, GUY et al. (2000), *Vers un nouveau contrat social*, Paris, Desclée de Brouwer.

SABOURIN, LOUIS (1996), "Inégalités et développement", in *The Study of Tensions Between Human Equality and Social Inequalities from the Perspectives of Various Social Sciences*, Proceedings of the First General Assembly of the Pontifical Academy of Social Sciences, Vatican City, pp. 141-163.

SABOURIN, LOUIS (2000), *La gouvernance globale, astuce passagère ou prémices d'un modèle de gestion en vue de mieux maîtriser la mondialisation?*, Treviso, International Institute Jacques Maritain.

SCHUMPETER, JOSEPH ALOIS (1967), *Theory of Economic Development, An Inquiry into Profits, Capital, Credit, Interest, and Business Cycle*, New York, Oxford University Press.

SECOND VATICAN COUNCIL (1965), Pastoral Constitution on the Church in the Modern World *Gaudium et Spes*, Vatican City.

TRUMAN, HARRY S. (1949), *Public Papers of the President of the United States*, 5, United States Government Printing Office.

UNITED NATIONS (1995), *The Copenhagen Declaration and Programme of Action / World Summit for Social Development*, New York.

UNITED NATIONS (1996), *Report of the World Summit for Social Development: Copenhagen 6-12 March 1995*, New York.

UNITED NATIONS (2000), *World Economic and Social Survey 2000, Trends and Policies in the World Economy*, Economic and Social Affairs Department, New York.

UNITED NATIONS RESEARCH INSTITUTE FOR SOCIAL DEVELOPMENT (1979), *Social Development and the International Strategy for Development*, Geneva.

What Now?, The 1975 Dag Hammarskjöld Report on Development and International Cooperation, published in the Journal of the Hammarskjöld Foundation, *Development Dialogue*, ½, 1975.

WORLD BANK (2000), *Poverty Reduction in the 1990s, An Evaluation of Strategy and Performance*, Washington, D.C., OED Publications.

WORLD BANK (2001), *World Development Report 2000/2001, Attacking poverty*, New York, Oxford University Press.

WORLD COMMISSION ON ENVIRONMENT AND DEVELOPMENT (1987), *Our Common Future*, Oxford, Oxford University Press.

HUMAN RIGHTS
AND THE DIGNITY OF THE PERSON

Dr. MARY ANN GLENDON *

Human rights and all that this phrase implies is based on the value of human dignity.

Eleanor Roosevelt [37]

When we speak of human rights, we are raising the fundamental question, what is man? And when we disagree about human rights, we are really disagreeing about the nature of the person.

Charles Malik [38]

During the two years it took them to draft the 1948 Universal Declaration of Human Rights, the members of the United Nations' first Human Rights Commission had surprisingly few discussions of why human beings have rights or why some rights are universal.[39] To men and women who had witnessed the horrors of two world wars, the need to affirm some minimal common standards of decency seemed evident. In haste to complete their work before the deepening Cold War destroyed its chance of acceptance by the General Assembly, the Declaration's framers did not linger on the problem of foundations.

At the Commission's first session in January 1947, however, Lebanon's representative, Charles Malik, did initiate a discussion about the premises on which such a document might be based.[40] A Christian Arab of the Greek Orthodox faith, Malik had been trained as a philosopher. His insistence on examining first principles precipitated the Commission's first argument, an intense dispute over the relation between man and society.

---

* Professor of Law at the Harvard University; Member of the Pontifical Academy of Social Sciences; Member of the Pontifical Council for the Laity.

[37] Quoted in STELLA HERSHAN, *A Woman of Quality*, New York, Crown, 1970, 248.

[38] Human Rights Commission, First Session, Summary Records (E/CN.4/SR 14, pp. 3-4).

[39] For details of the framing of the Universal Declaration, see MARY ANN GLENDON, *A World Made New: Eleanor Roosevelt and the Universal Declaration of Human Rights*, New York, Random House, 2001.

[40] Human Rights Commission, First Session, Summary Records (E/CN.4/SR 7, p. 4).

Malik began by asserting that, "When we speak of human rights, we are raising the fundamental question, what is man? And when we disagree about human rights, we are really disagreeing about the nature of the person". He then proposed four principles to guide the work of the Commission: First, the human person is more important than any national or cultural group to which he or she may belong. Second, a person's mind and conscience are his most sacred and inviolable possessions. Third, any pressure from the State, Church, or any other group aimed at coercing consent is unacceptable. Fourth, since groups, as well as individuals, may be right or wrong, the individual's freedom of conscience must be supreme.[41]

No sooner had Malik finished speaking than the Soviet bloc representatives denounced his proposed principles as completely unsuitable. All human rights, according to them, had to be seen in relation to the individual's obligations to the State which, as one of them put it, was "the main body which provides for man's existence, and the enjoyment of the human rights which belong to him". Malik responded that any sharp antithesis between the individual and society is artificial, since human beings are both individual and social. What is important, he said, is that the human person, though bound by social responsibilities, nevertheless has "the right to say no to any social pressure, and to legal protection of that right so that the person who dares to say no will not be physically eliminated".[42] The deepest danger of the present age, he argued, was "not that the State is not strong enough, ... but the danger posed by a collectivism [which demands] the extinction of the human person as such in his own individuality and ultimate inviolability".[43]

In the ensuing discussion, Malik's view on the over-riding importance of freedom of conscience was supported by the French member, René Cassin.[44] Cassin, a Zionist who described himself in his memoirs as a secular Jew, said, "This right is what gives man his value and dignity".[45] Eleanor Roosevelt, who chaired the eighteen-member group, weighed in on Malik's side, too. But she did so in a way that prompted Malik to point out an important difference in terminology. Mrs. Roosevelt habitually spoke of the primacy of

[41] Verbatim Record, in *The More Important Speeches and Interventions of Charles Malik* (Library of Congress, Manuscript Division), pp. 36-37; Human Rights Commission, First Session, Summary Records (E/CN.4/SR 14, pp. 3-4).

[42] *Ibid.*

[43] Verbatim Record, in *The More Important Speeches and Interventions of Charles Malik*, 35-37; Human Rights Commission, First Session, Summary Records (E/CN.4/SR 9, p. 3).

[44] Id. at 42-43.

[45] GLENDON, *A World Made New*, 61.

the "individual", whereas Malik said he preferred to use the word "person" in order to avoid connotations of radical autonomy and self-sufficiency.[46] As Alexis de Tocqueville wrote in the early nineteenth century, "individualism" was then a new word coined to express an idea that was beginning to flourish in democratic societies like the United States: "Individualism is a calm and considered feeling which disposes each citizen to isolate himself from the mass of his fellows and withdraw into the circle of family and friends: with this little society formed to his taste, he gladly leaves the greater society to look after itself".[47]

It was to avoid those connotations, and the more radical form of individualism that sets the individual apart even from the family, that Malik insisted on the word "person". The capacious notion of personhood — regarding the human being as uniquely valuable in himself, but as situated in the context of relationships — steers clear of the extremes of individualism and collectivism. That notion resonated across a broad spectrum of cultures — especially African, Asian, Latin American, and continental European. As a result, the Declaration's "Everyone" is not only a person whose individual dignity and rights must be respected. "Everyone" is also presented as situated in real-life relationships. The relationships specifically mentioned in the document include marriage, families, religious groups, workplace associations, political and social communities. A thick conception of personhood is so encoded in the Declaration that I am inclined to believe it is the document's hermeneutical key.

With hindsight, the Human Rights Commission's early debate on foundations marked a defining moment in the history of the UDHR. In later meetings, the question of the basis for human rights surfaced only sporadically. At the very end of the drafting process, and without much discussion, the Commissioners did approve a statement about the basis of human rights in the Preamble. The 1948 Declaration's opening line recites that "recognition of the inherent dignity and of the equal and inalienable rights of all members of the human family is the foundation of freedom, justice and peace in the world". The word "dignity" appears at so many key points in the Declaration that it can fairly be said to represent the Declaration's ultimate value. Human rights scholar Louis Henkin puts it this way: "Eschewing — in its quest for universality — explicit reliance on Divine inspiration or on

---

[46] Verbatim Record, in *The More Important Speeches and Interventions of Charles Malik*, 44.

[47] ALEXIS DE TOCQUEVILLE, *Democracy in America*, J.P. Mayer ed., New York, Doubleday Anchor, 1969, p. 506.

61

Natural Rights, the Declaration provided the idea of human rights with a universally acceptable foundation, an *ur* principle, human dignity".[48]

But in the post-modern era, the question arises: what is this "dignity", and what is *its* basis? The UN Charter professes "faith in freedom and democracy" which, according to the Charter, is grounded in another "faith" — "in the inherent dignity of men and women". That is a good deal of faith for a document that eschews divine inspiration. No wonder we find Nobel laureate Czeslaw Milosz musing ruefully about "those beautiful and deeply moving words which pertain to the old repertory of the rights of man and the dignity of the person".[49] Milosz probes further: "I wonder at this phenomenon because maybe underneath there is an abyss. After all, these ideas had their foundation in religion, and I am not over-optimistic as to the survival of religion in a scientific-technological civilization. Notions that seemed buried forever have suddenly been resurrected. But how long will they stay afloat if the bottom is taken out?".

Does the universal rights idea float above an abyss? Is it merely based on a kind of existential leap of faith? Or does it have some sturdier basis? Such questions have acquired increasing urgency in recent years as the Universal Declaration has come under attack from diverse quarters. Many of its critics describe the Declaration as an attempt to universalize a particular "Western" set of ideas and to impose them upon people who were under colonial rule and thus not represented in its creation. They dismiss the international human rights project as an instrument of "cultural imperialism" or "neo-colonialism". Although such charges are often made in bad faith, they serve as reminders of the need to place the claim of universality on firmer foundations.

That point was well understood by the members of a Committee on the Theoretical Bases for Human Rights that was convened by UNESCO in 1947 to look into the question of whether any rights could be said to be universal and, if so, what those rights might be. The group was composed of many of the world's leading thinkers, including the French Catholic philosopher Jacques Maritain who was one of its most active members. After consulting dozens of other philosophers and religious thinkers from Eastern and Western cultures, the UNESCO group discovered to its surprise that a few basic practical concepts of humane conduct were so widely shared that

[48] Louis Henkin, "Human Rights: Ideology and Aspiration, Reality and Prospect," in *Realizing Human Rights*, Samantha Power and Graham Allison eds., New York, St. Martin's Press, 2000, 3.

[49] Czeslaw Milosz, "The Religious Imagination at 2000", *New Perspectives Quarterly*, Fall 1997, 32.

they could plausibly "be viewed as implicit in man's nature as a member of society".[50] Dignity, freedom, tolerance and neighborliness, they found, were highly prized in many cultural and religious traditions — even though the elaboration of these concepts as "rights" was a relatively modern, and European, phenomenon.

Though the UNESCO philosophers found that a few basic norms of decent human behavior were widely shared, they were aware that different nations and cultures attach quite different weights to these norms. They realized, too, that differing political and economic conditions would affect each nation's ability to bring human rights principles to life. They did not, however, regard those facts as fatal to the universality of human rights. They never envisioned that a common standard of achievement would or should produce completely uniform practices.[51]

The framers of the Universal Declaration followed the UNESCO philosophers in rejecting the notion that universal principles must be implemented in the same way everywhere. The Chinese member of the drafting committee, Confucian philosopher P. C. Chang, stressed that point in his December 9, 1948 speech to the General Assembly urging adoption of the Declaration. He deplored that colonial powers had tried to impose on other peoples a standardized way of thinking and a single way of life. That sort of uniformity could only be achieved, he said, by force or at the expense of truth. It could never last.[52] Chang and his colleagues on the drafting committee expected the Declaration's rights would be inculturated in various ways, and that over time the corpus of human rights would be enriched by these varied experiences. As a distinguished international lawyer wrote on the document's thirty-fifth anniversary, "The Declaration does not purport to offer a single unified conception of the world as it should be, nor does it purport to offer some sort of comprehensive recipe for the attainment of an ideal world. Its purpose is rather the more modest one of proclaiming a set of values which are capable of giving some guidance to modern society in choosing among a wide range of alternative policy options".[53]

---

[50] RICHARD P. McKEON, "The Philosophic Bases and Material Circumstances of the Rights of Man", in *Human Rights: Comments and Interpretations*, New York, Columbia University Press, 1949, 45.

[51] JACQUES MARITAIN, "Introduction", in *Human Rights: Comments and Interpretations*, 16.

[52] Plenary Meetings of the General Assembly, 181st Plenary Meeting, December 10, 1948, p. 895.

[53] PHILIP ALSTON, "The Universal Declaration at 35: Western and Passé or Alive and Universal?", *International Commission of Jurists Review*, July 1983, 60, 69.

To help assure fidelity to the Declaration's principles as the process of inculturation unfolds, the framers endowed the Declaration with an interpretive matrix: freedom and solidarity, grounded in the dignity of the human person.[54] By the 1970s, however, the original understanding of the Declaration was already largely forgotten. And what oblivion had not erased, opportunism was eroding. The abstentions by South Africa and Saudi Arabia from the final vote approving the Declaration had been early signals of possible trouble ahead. South Africa had objected to the word "dignity", fearing its implications for the apartheid system she was then constructing. And Saudi Arabia, alone among the nations with large Islamic populations, had claimed that some of the Declaration's rights, particularly the right to change one's religion, were really just "Western" ideas.

In 1948, those were isolated claims. But as time passed and as the Cold War antagonists pulled apart and politicized the provisions of the UDHR, the stage was set for a broader assault on the idea of universal human rights and dignity. In 1955, the charge that the Declaration was an instrument of "Western" neo-colonialism resurfaced with particular vehemence at the Bandoeng Conference, where the "non-aligned" nations found unity of a sort in shared resentment of the dominance of a few rich and powerful countries in world affairs. Then, in the 1960s and 1970s, threats to the integrity of the UDHR appeared within the human rights movements of the West. Those movements were deeply influenced by the highly individualistic ideas about rights that predominated in the United States in those years,[55] and they attracted many special interest groups who were more interested in harnessing the Declaration's moral authority to their own agendas than in furthering its original purposes. Activists, including some affiliated with the UN, began to speak of "reinventing" human rights, of a "radical reinterpretation of the earlier generation of rights",[56] and of "deconstructing and reconfiguring the human rights framework".[57]

[54] For demonstration of this point with textual references, see GLENDON, *A World Made New*, Chapter 10.

[55] See generally, MARY ANN GLENDON, *Rights Talk*, New York, Free Press, 1991 (especially Chapter 6); ANTHONY LESTER, "The Overseas Trade in the American Bill of Rights", 88 *Columbia Law Review* 537, 1988.

[56] E.g., RADHIKA COOMARASWAMY (UN Special Rapporteur on Violence Against Women), *Reinventing International Law: Women's Rights as Human Rights in the International Community*, Harvard Law School Human Rights Program, 1997, 20, 25.

[57] BERTA HERNANDEZ-TRUYOL, "Women's Rights as Human Rights – Rules, Realities and the Role of Culture: A Formula for Reform", 21 *Brooklyn Journal of International Law*, 1996, 605, 607.

The process of deconstruction of the UDHR — dis-aggregating its provisions, promoting selected rights, and downplaying others in line with the agenda of whatever group was doing the reinterpreting — was facilitated by the now-well-established habit of reading the Declaration in the way that Americans read their Bill of Rights, that is, as a string of essentially separate guarantees. The Declaration's dignitarian, personalist language of rights began to be displaced by the more simplistic kinds of rights talk that were then making deep inroads on political discourse in the United States. Several features of that new rights dialect had the potential to wreak havoc with the Declaration: rights envisioned without individual or social responsibilities, one's favorite rights touted as absolute with others ignored; the rights-bearer imagined as radically autonomous and self-sufficient; the trivialization of core freedoms by special interests posing as new rights.[58]

For decades, the holistic nature of the Declaration has been ignored by its professed supporters as well as by its attackers. By isolating each part from its place in the overall design, the now-common misreading of the Declaration promotes misunderstanding and facilitates misuse. Nations and interest groups ignore the provisions they find inconvenient and treat others as trumps. One major casualty has been the Declaration's vision of the rights-bearer as a person situated in relationships. Another has been its insistence on the links between freedom and solidarity (just at a time when affluent nations seem increasingly to be washing their hands of poor countries and peoples). Thus, ironically, the charge of cultural imperialism has acquired more credibility. The global spread of hyper-libertarian, radically individualistic, sound-bite rights ideas has rendered the contemporary international human rights project more vulnerable to the label of "Western" than the Declaration ever was.

That there might be some such demolition derby in the Declaration's future was foreseen long ago by Richard McKeon, the Rapporteur of the UNESCO philosophers' commission. McKeon realized what every lawyer knows: practical agreements such as those reached by the UN member States in 1948 are achieved only at the price of a certain ambiguity. The same generality that made agreement possible, however, rendered the document more vulnerable to misunderstanding and manipulation. In his UNESCO report, McKeon pointed out that different understandings of the meanings of rights usually reflect divergent concepts of man and of society which in turn cause the persons who hold those understandings to

---

[58] See generally, GLENDON, *Rights Talk*. On the need for care in accepting new rights, see PHILIP ALSTON, "Conjuring up New Rights: A Proposal for Quality Control", 78 *American Journal of International Law* 607, 1984.

have different views of reality. Thus, he predicted accurately that "difficulties will be discovered in the suspicions, suggested by these differences, concerning the tangential uses that might be made of a declaration of human rights for the purpose of advancing special interests".[59]

As memories fade about why the nations of the world determined, after two world wars, to affirm certain basic rights as universal, efforts to deconstruct the Universal Declaration and remake it nearer to the heart's desire of this or that special interest group can be expected to increase. Whether the dignitarian vision of freedom and solidarity in the Universal Declaration can withstand the combined stresses of aggressive lobbying, heightened national and ethnic assertiveness, and the powerful, ambiguous forces of globalization, is impossible to foresee. Not only UN agencies, but the governments of several liberal democracies have become implicated in breaking down the connections among its indivisible rights, deconstructing the core principle of human dignity and ignoring its nuanced conception of human personhood and relationships.

The ongoing contests for control of the meaning of the Declaration are forceful reminders of the need to attend to the unfinished business of foundations. As Pope John Paul II pointed out in his Address to the Vatican Diplomatic Corps in January 1989, "[T]he 1948 Declaration does not contain the anthropological and moral bases for the human rights that it proclaims" (7).

Fortunately, that work has begun.[60] Those who are laboring within their various traditions to develop the missing foundations, however, are doing so under the gaze of profound skeptics. It is not only the critical theorists of the left and the hard-boiled "realists" of the right who maintain that the Declaration is incoherent or that the meaning of its principles is indeterminate. The late Michel Villey, for example, could see no solution to the problem that, "Each of the so-called human rights is the negation of other human rights, and when practiced separately generates *injustices*".[61] Another Christian philosopher, Alasdair MacIntyre, argues that different rights, borrowed from

---

[59] RICHARD McKEON, "The Philosophic Bases and Material Circumstances of the Rights of Man", in *Human Rights: Comments and Interpretations*, 35, 36.

[60] See, e.g., the path-breaking work by THOMAS WILLIAMS, *Rights and the Person: An Inquiry into the Foundations of Human Rights in the Light of Thomistic Personalism* (forthcoming). For references to works in various religious, cultural and philosophical traditions, see GLENDON, *A World Made New,* p. 268, n. 7.

[61] MICHEL VILLEY, *Le droit et les droits de l'homme*, Paris, Presses Universitaires de France, 1983, 13.

different traditions, often rest on different, and incommensurable, moral premises.[62]

The UNESCO philosophers, however, took a view that was more pragmatic, as well as more sanguine. Maritain pointed out, anticipating Villey's objection, that, as a matter of common sense, "If each of the human rights were by its nature absolutely unconditional and exclusive of any limitation, ... obviously any conflict between them would be irreconcilable. But who does not know in reality that these rights, being human, are ... subject to conditioning and limitation, at least where their exercise is concerned? That the various rights ascribed to the human being limit each other, particularly that the ... rights of man as a person involved in the life of the community cannot be given room in human history without restricting, to some extent, the freedoms and rights of man as an individual person, is only normal".[63]

Maritain went on to note that, "Where difficulties and arguments begin is in the determination of the scale of values governing the exercise and concrete integration of these various rights".[64] The Declaration would thus need some "ultimate value whereon those rights depend and in terms of which they are integrated by mutual limitations". That value in the UDHR, as in many post-World War II constitutions, is the dignity of the human person.[65]

But it has become painfully apparent that the shift from nature to dignity in modern thinking about the foundations of human rights entails certain difficulties that inevitably lead back to the question of the human person. Dignity, we have learned, possesses no more immunity to manipulation than any other concept. One need only think of current defenses of active euthanasia in terms of an alleged "right to die with dignity".

The common secular understandings are that human beings have dignity because they are autonomous beings capable of making choices (Kant), or because of the sense of empathy that most human beings feel for other sentient creatures (Rousseau). But the former understanding has alarming implications for persons of diminished capacity, and the latter places all morality on the fragile basis of a transient feeling. Persons of religious faith

[62] ALASDAIR MacINTYRE, *After Virtue*, Notre Dame, Notre Dame University Press, 1981, 2, 8.

[63] JACQUES MARITAIN, *Man and the State*, Chicago, University of Chicago Press, 1951, 106.

[64] JACQUES MARITAIN, "Introduction", in *Human Rights: Comments and Interpretations*, 9, 15-16.

[65] See, for example, Art. 1 of the *German Basic Law*: "Human dignity is inviolable. To respect and protect it is the duty of all state authority".

may believe that dignity is grounded in the fact that human beings are made in the image and likeness of God, but that proposition is not accepted by nonbelievers.

Even for Christian believers, moreover, the path from dignity to human rights is not clear and straight. Philosopher Brian Benestad has pointed out that the term "dignity of the human person" has two different connotations in Christian teaching: "It is both a given and an achievement to be gradually realized".[66] The Catholic Catechism, he notes, begins its discussion of morality with this quotation from Pope Leo the Great: "Christian, recognize your dignity, and now that you share in God's own nature, do not return by sin to your former base condition".

Now, if dignity is a quality to be achieved by strenuous effort, it is not self-evident that the dignity of the rights claimant is an adequate basis for human rights. After all, not every rights claimant has made strenuous efforts to overcome sin. From a Christian point of view, the resolution of this dilemma may be that human rights are grounded in the obligation of everyone to perfect one's own dignity which in turn obliges us to respect the "given" spark of dignity in others (whatever they have done with it). In other words, it may be our own quest for dignity (individually and as members of society) that requires us to refrain from cruelty and neglect toward our fellow human beings.

In that light, the drafters of the UN Charter were prudent to say that human rights rest upon a "faith" in human dignity. It would be a mistake, however, to leap from that proposition to the notion that faith is merely an act of will, an arbitrary or existential choice. Ongoing work in the world's great religious and philosophical traditions reveals that those traditions can furnish compelling reasons for respecting the dignity of all members of the human family — that faith and reason do indeed work together to elevate the soul of man.

The unfinished business ahead, however, is not only intellectual, but cultural. As Maritain put it, many kinds of music can be played on the Declaration's thirty strings, but whether that music is "in tune with, or harmful to, human dignity" will depend primarily on the extent to which a "culture of human dignity develops".[67] Since religion is at the heart of culture, Dr. Giorgio Filibeck of the Pontifical Council for Justice and Peace has rightly pointed out that a great challenge faces the world's religions: it will be

[66] BRIAN BENESTAD, "Do Today's Catholics Know Anything About the Church's Social Teachings?", in *Keeping Faith: Msgr. George Kelly's Battle for the Church*, Patrick Reilly ed., Front Royal, VA, Christendom Press, 2000, pp. 31-61.
[67] JACQUES MARITAIN, "Introduction" at 16.

68

up to them to show that they are capable of motivating their followers to perfect their own dignity and to respect the dignity of others.[68] And since the transformation of culture begins with the transformation of persons, one by one, there seems to be no escape from the conclusion that respect for human dignity begins at home — in the heart and mind of each and every person.

April 2002

[68] GIORGIO FILIBECK, "Universal Religions and the Universality of Human Rights", Presentation at the Harvard Law School World Alumni Congress Panel on "Religion and Human Rights", held at the Islamic Center of Rome, Italy, June 11, 1998.

DEMOCRACY, HUMAN RIGHTS AND THE RULE OF LAW: THE "TRINITY" OF POLITICS

Dr. JANNE HAALAND MATLARY*

Democracy is the Only Legitimate Form of Government Today

Democracy is one justified form of government where legitimacy emanates from the people. The legacy of liberal democracy is the normative model for most European States, and is the only acceptable form of government in the West today. Even among self-professed sceptics who hold that no values or norms are universal, one is hard pressed to find a critic of democracy as such. All agree that this form of government is the best one, or at least the best there is in the absence of Platonic philosophers of the real kind. Democracy has come to stay and has developed in the West over the last two to three hundred years. It is perhaps the only concept that is openly spoken of in Western politics as something that all should enjoy: one states that democracy must be instituted all over the world.

This form of government gradually included the whole population over a certain age by extending suffrage to them. It is characterised by having representative institutions and holding periodic elections. Elected politicians are accountable to the electorate and can be "recalled" in a new election. The government is accountable to Parliament and there is a formal separation of powers in the legislative, the executive and the judiciary. The constitution contains a Bill of Rights that lists fundamental rights of citizens — typically the right to life, liberty, property, the right to freedom of religion, association and free speech. The French and American constitutions serve as models for many European constitutions.

Typically these basic norms are regarded as "higher" than other law and as so fundamental that they cannot easily be changed. Parliaments thus have elaborate and cumbersome procedures for changing constitutions. In some countries there are special constitutional courts that are in charge of interpreting what the constitution really says. In short, modern democracies are equipped with a *code of higher norms* that are supposed to be safe from political change and which are therefore insulated from the political process.

* Professor of International Politics, University of Oslo; Member of the Pontifical Council for Justice and Peace; Consultor of the Pontifical Council for the Family.

Democracy is Based on Higher Norms

How were these norms generated? Where did they come from? In the French civil code they were simply decided on, as they were in other constitutions. For John Locke, the father of modern democratic theory, the fundamental norms were self-evident. He held that there were some higher norms which could not be reasoned about. But they were generated in the establishment of the "social contract" and were thus not "pre-political", belonging to man as a human being.

Modern democratic theory arose as part of social contract theory and rests on three assumptions. First, that there are self-evident rights that belong to the individual and which should be protected by the constitution. These rights are however only postulated as such; they are not part of any argument about natural law. Second, the need for protection of these postulated rights is the reason for the creation of society in a social contract: in the state of nature, man is thought to pursue self-interest in the form of power maximation but he needs to be protected from the others. Third, the State is a minimalist arbiter of pluralism among atomistic individuals: the State carries no values, politics is value-neutral. This institutional apparatus is what largely constitutes the legacy of modern democracy in the West.

The Danger of Tyranny of the Majority

But when there is no agreement on the higher norms or standards in a democracy, and even a denial that such can exist, we face the classical problem of tyranny of the majority. This refers to the situation where democracy degenerates into being simply the will of the majority in each and every matter, and where no high norms are accepted as real. The idea of a *Rechtsstaat* implies that the decisions of the majority will always be checked against these higher constitutional norms. However, this is a relatively weak tradition in Western democracies today, save for Germany. In all States we see a tendency for the majority in Parliament to decide on political matters that really concern human rights, such as abortion and euthanasia, both instances of the first of human rights, the right to life. However, these issues are redefined to divest them of this classification, to be discussed below.

Mill, Tocqueville, and others were, over a century back, extremely concerned with the problem of majority tyranny. Mill's *On Liberty* (1859), the classic plea for liberty as the highest norm, agonises over this issue:

"Protection against the tyranny of the magistrate is not enough; there needs to be protection also against the tyranny of the prevailing opinion and feeling ... against the tendency of society to impose ... its own ideas and practices as rules of conduct on those who dissent from them ... There is a limit to the interference of collective opinion with individual independence, and to find that limit is as indispensable to a good condition of human affairs as protection against political despotism".

On the one hand, Mill saw the emergence of such a tyranny in democracy, on the other hand he could not find any remedy against it. This was because his premises were inconsistent: he postulated tolerance or liberty as the highest norm, saying that all is allowed that does not harm others. Politics is value-neutral, and only if you harm others should your freedom not be allowed. Yet he clearly held that some actions and norms are right and true, whereas others are wrong, but could not argue for this as he had no criterion of ranking value-judgements. The interpretation of what does harm and what does not ultimately rests with subjective opinion. Since the State has to somehow decide in these cases, it is unavoidable that politics embodies values and is about value-judgements.

Mill's problem is the same that we face today: Tolerance or liberty is almost the only norm that democracy accepts and is certainly the highest norm. We see this all the time in the public debate: new interest groups claim freedom from interference, claim tolerance for their interests, whatever the moral content of them. Morals or ethics is thought to belong to the private sphere and to be subjectivistic. Value pluralism is the key premise.

Given this, how can — if at all — fundamental norms be safeguarded? The procedure of democracy is some form of majority voting. Even constitutions can be changed by parliaments, although the procedures are more cumbersome than simple majority and take more time. However, the basic premise is that all political power is vested in the people, who in a social contract invests it in the institutions of State. Even the rights in the constitution come from the people, it would seem. But is this the case? Here we see an inherent inconsistency between the "self-evident" character of fundamental individuals' rights, which are simply postulated, and the tendency today to usurp these rights by changing them through majority voting. I will return to empirical illustrations of this.

Classical democracy conceived of constitutional rights as being beyond the reach of majority procedure, although the constitutions themselves could be changed. The judiciary was designed to be independent of the legislature in order to interpret and protect the constitution. However, the crux of the matter with regard to law and politics is not in variants of institutional design, but in the view of the origin of law. If all is reducible to politics, there can be no protection from the application of the majority procedure to any principled question of human rights.

The autonomy of the private sphere is essential to democracy, as is the respect for civil disobedience in cases of conflict between an individual's norms and those of society. However, this is not enough. The State in the classical model was a minimal State whose role it was to deal with the tasks that the private sphere could not rationally solve by itself: army, police, postal, energy and infrastructure services. The historical evolution of the State has led to a much larger public sphere, the development of the welfare State, and to State schools and often State churches. Whatever one's views on this development, it is clear that a sound democracy must contain a private sector with autonomous associations, a free market, and some distance between politics and the law. Further, it must recognise the premise of equality before the law, as well as in political participation.

The major problem of modern Western democracy is the reduction of ethical questions to pragmatic, political ones. This is manifested in the lack of respect for human life in its non-utilitarian forms: unborn, handicapped, old and sick; and in subjecting the taking of human life to pragmatic decision-making by majority procedure. This empirical development shows that the right to life enshrined in constitutions and international human rights documents carries little if any weight when pitted against feminist, economic or other interests. More importantly, it shows that modern democracy is reduced to majority procedure. With tolerance as the only professed norm of the State, majority procedure becomes the essence of democracy. This development is inconsistent with the *Rechtsstaatstradition* which is based on the primacy of higher, unchangeable norms and independent institutions to safeguard them.

Some Empirical Examples

Abortion came to the fore in the public debate in Western democracies some 30 years ago. Everyone knew that abortions had always been performed, in secrecy in the private sphere. Now women demanded that the State should perform them. Their argument was pragmatic: abortions will happen; they should be made "safe". Abortion was politicised, i.e. placed in the public-political sphere, by feminist interest groups.

The terms of the debate had to be pragmatic because the liberal State cannot deal with "value" questions. The State does not represent norms — the constitutional norms are just there to protect the individual from intrusion into his private sphere. The decision-making procedure in liberal democracy is majority decision. If, however, the terms of the debate are about universal norms of right and wrong, this procedure makes no sense. The political discussion thus has to be set in other terms. It has to be pragmatic.

In the case of the abortion debate, *the fierce struggle which continues and which will continue is about the terms of the debate*. If the question is, "under which conditions can human life be taken?", one has to consider the constitutional norms of right to life and the international instruments of human rights that state this as the highest norm. If the debate is cast in pragmatic terms, e.g. as a women's issue, this is not necessary. *The abortion issue was decided when the terms of the debate were decided.* But abortion represents a water-shed in Western politics precisely because it exhibits a total cleavage in views on what is legitimate democratic politics and procedure.

This meant that principled reasoning was defined away and that interest group politics won out. The same political process can be seen in the debate over *euthanasia*, which is now becoming politically prominent in Scandinavia, Australia, the U.S., and gradually in other Western States. The terms of the debate are being set in a very important process right now. For instance, one sees reports in the press on the increasing number of people that favour euthanasia, doctors who find it good for the patient, euthanasia as the right to choose, it is a new human right, etc. Interest group leaders actually say things like, "We do not have enough resources for all people; we must put priority on the young" (*Aftenposten*, March 1996). There is in other words a process going on that seeks to *pragmatise* the issue so that it can easily be decided by majority opinion, and a concomitant process driven by interest groups that argues that abortion and euthanasia are new *human rights*.

A third issue that illustrates the inability to discuss ethical issues in ethical terms, is that of using *foetal tissue* from induced abortion for medical purposes. In Norway an expert commission was set up to advise the government on this issue. Even the one bishop on the commission — a member of the Lutheran State Church — turned out to be sympathetic to the government's proposal to use such tissue medically. The interesting aspect of this was however his way of reasoning: being against legalised abortion, he nonetheless argued for the use of foetal tissue because, as abortion is allowed, one might as well make use of the results of it. He could not understand that there were problems with this argument from an ethical point of view — and in truth, his was a valid pragmatic argument: abortions will happen, let's make some use of them if we can. He could not understand that if he held that abortions were evil on principle, he would also have to hold that the ancillary act, using the foetal tissue, was evil and in fact might contribute to justifying the abortion itself.

These examples illustrate that the political discourse on ethical issues in liberal democracy is *de facto* pragmatic. Moreover, I have argued that *it has to be* pragmatic in order to fit with the central assumptions and institutions of liberal democracy: majority procedure, politics as "value-free", and ethics as belonging to the private sphere. Yet it is also cast in "rights" language — the right of women to abort, the right of old people to euthanasia, and so on.

But the "rights" language is justified by pragmatic reasoning: because women have abortions, they are a right; and because many people accept euthanasia, it is a right. In this debate there is no discussion of which topics should belong in the private sphere — the strategy is to lift them into the public sphere. There is no hierarchy of principles for determining what is a common, and thus political problem, and what is not. We are faced with a completely confused debate, driven by interest groups.

How pervasive is this development? Abortion has become a "right" in many Western countries and continues to make "progress" beyond Europe. Euthanasia is legalised in several countries already and I am convinced that it is only a question of time before it will be legal. The "rights" language used to make these policies more acceptable destroys the notion of fundamental constitutional rights by denying that there can be a hierarchy of rights and even that there are fundamental contradictions between rights, such as the right to life and the right to abortion.

Solutions?

I have argued that, judged on the norms of constitutionalism — that there are fundamental norms laid down in the constitution — , contemporary democratic practice is often tyrannical. I say "practice" because the institutions of liberal democracy have not been changed. One simply elevates the majority procedure to become the cornerstone of democracy and conveniently forgets the constitutional constraints on its exercise.

Further, there is no longer any shared "values" or norms. The central premise of "neutrality" on the part of the State in normative questions has of course always been a fiction. States act on norms in most of what they do as modern welfare States: they inculcate pupils with national and social norms in national school systems and they decide redistribution, health and foreign policies according to moral or normative standpoints.

The postulation of tolerance as the hallmark of the modern State is also fiction — it is a tolerance very selectively applied indeed. In questions of the taking of human life, as in abortion and euthanasia, one does not ask the logical ethical question of "when is the taking of human life justified?". Here the State has no normative stand even if its constitution explicitly states that a right to life exists. In these cases one avoids the normative discussion altogether and opts for a combination of pragmatism ("there is a need for abortion, abortions happen all the time") and selective "rights" language (since abortions are favoured by a majority, a "right" to abortion exists). The fallacy of inferring the existence of a right from empirical data is obvious, but hardly seen as such.

Here we are at the very core of the problem of democracy and value relativism. The two cannot meaningfully coexist: democracies where there is no set of fundamental norms underlying the political process become, sooner or later, tyrannies. Above I have pointed to the institutional inconsistencies within liberal democracy and the abuses of this system today. But the main problem is not institutional, it is ethical.

"Values" connote subjectivity: "I accept abortion, you do not" — our value preferences differ. "I accept euthanasia, you do not". Again, simply a matter of different preferences. "I accept genocide, you do not".

But do we agree with this statement? No — here the reaction will be one of universal condemnation of killing for ethnic reasons. This shows two things: one, in dealing with the question of taking human life, the public is inconsistent because the question is not posed as one of principle, i.e. of ethics; and two, there is still a sound reaction in most people about genocide. They will not hesitate to condemn it as evil — but if values are simply subjective preferences, they ought logically to say "I don't happen to like genocide, but if you do, you simply have other preferences than I".

There thus exists a remnant of the language of morals in people. One reacts to dictatorships by calling them "unjust", and thus retains some notion of justice. Justice was the basis for all legitimate government in the classical tradition, and justice requires principled reasoning. "When can human life justifiably be taken?" Traditionally the answer was "in self-defence". The lost discourse on ethics today points back to much richer European tradition of natural law, developed by Aristotle, rediscovered by St. Thomas and further developed by him and medieval Christian thinkers. This discourse on politics disappeared with the triumph of the language of "*Staatsraison*" at the time of Machiavelli. Here one no longer discussed the relationship between "might and right", but rather how to gain and keep "might". The question of justice as right ordering of society became obsolete.

We have seen that the utilitarianism of a Mill or Locke, coupled with the institutions of liberal democracy, invite the conclusion that "might becomes right". There is no higher norm outside of politics. Likewise, with a Kantian approach one logically safeguards fundamental human rights, but these rights do not come from man's nature; they remain a postulate that is in the interest of all in a civilised polity.

My contention is that only an anthropology that starts with the absolute dignity of the human being — of *any* human being — will do to ensure that persons will not be treated in a utilitarian manner. However, the problem is how to make the dignity of man apparent to all in societies where the word dignity no longer carries any meaning and where Nietzsche's *Umwertung aller Werte* is the point of departure. In academia in most of the Western world today it makes no sense to speak of a universal human nature, and thus of universal norms. Where this is impossible, the whole Western discourse on justice collapses.

My clear impression is that today the very idea of someone claiming *truth* value for something — as do all religions — is met with the reaction that the idea of truth itself is intolerant and undemocratic. If something is true, it implies that something else is untrue. Today this seems somehow intolerant: that there can be truth, and that this truth can be discovered. It is far easier to create God in one's own image.

Thus, there is a tremendous *tension* between Western public opinion and Christianity. This should be recognised. I think the "solution" is to have enough space for religious practice and public expression: Christians claim truth, Muslims claim truth, Jews claim truth, atheists claim truth — and they all coexist in a pluralist democracy. At a recent seminar on religious freedom, someone, an agnostic, said: "Then all religions must stop claiming truth and find some compromise". This led to a scream from all the religious people present, and they represented all the religions I mentioned: What an utterly stupid and unrealistic proposal! This chap has not understood that one's religious conviction is far more important than anything else in life.

The "solution" is that truth claims can exist in democracy. Democracy is not about the ultimate issues in life, such as the meaning of life and the existence of God. It is about a minimal common ground in norms and morals so that problems can be solved and pluralism can blossom. It is also an arena for discussion and offers an openness that we have never before had in history for debating religious issues. But it must be based on some common values, and these can be found in the UN Declaration of Human Rights of 1948, which expresses a view of the human person which is compatible with Christian social teaching and natural law.

77

A Practical Way Ahead

How can one, as a citizen, start to address these issues in the contemporary political debate? It is easy to diagnose the problem as one where pragmatism overtakes human dignity and principled human rights consideration, it is quite another to try to influence society in another direction. However, the social teaching is a practical teaching, aimed at action. I have therefore reflected much on how one can start to change current democracy in the direction of a society based more on an integral view of human dignity than on *ad hoc* pragmatism.

I would say that there are *four areas* of special importance where one must start to work and apply principled considerations. Here there are very good international human rights standards as well as an elaborate, rich social teaching.

The most critical areas are, in my view, respect for human dignity as an absolute value; support for the family; respect for freedom of religion and churches; and national as well as international solidarity, also across generations.

Let me attach some few comments to each of these areas:

Human dignity: Today we see a particularly utilitarian tendency to view others in terms of their usefulness to us. We worship youth, beauty, effectiveness and achievement in our societies. The old and the sick are sometimes barely tolerated. The unborn are invisible and therefore do not count, and the same goes for the old and sick. As family ties become less important in society, these people are thought to be the concern of the State rather than of us. It is very easy to rob them of their respect, which is their due as human beings.

We must help society regain respect for the human person. This is the only way to combat abortion and euthanasia, as well as all other inroads made against human dignity in the field of genetic engineering and bioethics.

We must restore the sense of mystery and sacredness about the human person so that people will realise that a human being is infinitely more than a heap of flesh and bones. There is a beauty, often hidden, about an old person or a sick person, but only an eye that sees the individual beyond the body can discover this. All of us, at one time or another, realise that the other is our *Mitmensch* — our brother in a very real sense. Yet this ability to recognise all others as fellow human beings must be trained and cultivated, lest it die in us.

I think the Christian in politics must act as a constant reminder of the *existential fellowship* of all persons, regardless of circumstances. We must not remain indifferent to our brothers and sisters; yet it is very easy to show solidarity only with our kin.

We *cannot hope* for any new and more fruitful debate on abortion and euthanasia unless we succeed in this. After three decades of abortion on demand in my country I find that most people are completely indifferent to the humanhood of the foetus before three months gestational age. It simply does not exist. Likewise, there is a large and growing indifference to old people — they are marginalised in terms of influence anyway. There are a tremendous number of lonely old people around.

Politically this means both a principled defence of all human life and an insistence on such a principled discussion in national politics. This requires that abortion, euthanasia and other issues in bioethics that relate to the taking or changing of human life be dealt with as the same kind of issues, within their international context of human rights. They cannot be addressed at the national level only, although that is what we see happening in most States.

We must also be very aware of the tendency to talk about abortion and euthanasia as the only instances of disrespect for human dignity. We must never confine our concern to these extreme instances only. We are not credible in our defence of human dignity unless we also include a *general* commitment to solidarity with all, not least in the economic sense.

This brings me to the second issue, *solidarity*. Human dignity is not respected if we allow for large discrepancies in economic and social welfare. Today market liberalism and its corollary, consumerism, are the key problems. There is the infamous gap which is widening between poor and rich States; but there is also more and more power vested in market actors to the detriment of political actors. We see this in global capitalism and within each European State.

The labour side has lost bargaining power because capital has become global, and employers increasingly hire or lay off people with the *hausse* and the *baisse* of the stocks. There seems to be no *ethos* whatsoever left on the part of the employer — short-term profit and not development that benefits employers and community alike, seems to be the only motive. This in turn makes it almost impossible for an employee to settle down and plan a family.

In my view capital has far too much power today. It is known that the old socialist welfare State did not work, but we must not rescind on the concept of the welfare State. There is a clear need for the State to redistribute in order to attain economic justice within society. For instance, I find it unacceptable that one's parents' income — and not hard work and talent — should decide whether one can go to university; or that a pregnant woman should be unable to have her child because there is no social allowance. Likewise, there is a clear need to sustain families when they cannot provide enough income through work, or when unemployment happens.

But the picture today in Europe is bleak in this respect: economic differences are widening, and jobs are less secure than before. There has not been a good replacement to socialism in terms of welfare State thinking apart from Catholic social teaching. We need to put that teaching into practice.

Internationally, donor fatigue is rising. Fewer and fewer give less and less development assistance. In addition, the values of materialism dominate us. It is indeed hard for a mother like me to fight the influence of the market on my children.

Christians must live solidarity in all aspects of life. Wealth creation must not be for oneself and one's family only, but for the whole human community. Further, wealth is only a means, not an end, like all material possessions.

This is a hard lesson to practice. Most of us are very interested in material comfort and ownership. It gives an easy life and it gives status. We all desire this or that, and have to fight this dominant tendency all the time. For non-Christians it is even more difficult to realise that things are but a means to something else.

Today there is tremendous power in the market, and concomitantly less power in politics. We must fight to regain political power because the political is about the ordering of all of society, to which economics must be subordinate. With globalisation, this is much more difficult than in the era of the nation-state.

But power comes to politics if and when we put our energy into it, disregarding our own private concerns about wealth. We can and must invest power in political institutions again — through the participation of all.

Christians must share in all senses, also in the economic one. There is no mistake about the preference Christ had for the poor. Indeed, he was also one of them.

Further, in terms of democracy there is no doubt that the equality on which it rests, equality in terms of human dignity, also implies a certain economic equality. Here the social teaching is strong and sophisticated, and a voice that is rare in the neoclassical paradigm of the current political debate.

The third area which is important in politics is the *family*. Today there are several challenges to the health of the family: unemployment and job insecurity for young people who are about to start a family; less political support for families and thus a weaker position for this institution; and a massive increase in divorces as well as individualism. It is no longer a foregone conclusion that one will marry and have a family, and the very concept of the family is itself being challenged.

We record that birth rates in Europe are very low, especially in Spain and Italy, but also in Eastern Europe. I like to boast that Norway has the highest birth rate in Europe, and this is due to good social policies like a one-year paid maternity leave, paternity leave and job security for the mother when she returns to employment. The politicians in Europe must realise that today women are as well or even better educated than men, and that they consequently both *want* to work — and usually *have* to work for economic reasons.

The old sex role pattern has definitely changed with the educational revolution. If women lose their jobs when they have children, they are not going to have children.

In order to make it possible for the family to survive in Europe, we must have strong social and economic policies that protect it. Fathers must take their rightful share of housework and responsibility for the family.

But this is of great *urgency* in European politics — already there is far too low a birth rate to sustain the population, to mention but one important aspect. The very concept of democracy assumes that there is a *polis* of commonweal, of common interests. Unless there are families that form the smallest and most basic societies in the larger society, we are faced with a collection of atomistic individuals that together have little community.

Today there is, in addition to the economic problems for the family, also a tremendous individualism and little faith in the ability to stay married for a lifetime. Most people seem to want to try out marriage, or at least cohabitation, to see if it works, but not make any firm commitment. It is very easy to walk out, and this is fully accepted by society's norms today. Christians have a big challenge in trying to show the point of lifelong marriage. To most the idea sounds like a nightmare: to spend perhaps forty or fifty years with the same man or woman, losing one's precious freedom. How can anyone dare to make such vows? Why would anyone want to? Better to play it safe and retain the exit option.

A Norwegian author who has very much inspired me, Sigrid Undset, wrote as far back as in the 1920s that lenient marriage laws acted like a door that was always open, letting constant draft into the home. The temptation to leave was always there, presenting itself as perfectly acceptable. Today this draft is like a gale force wind: almost no one speaks for lifelong marriage in the public.

Children suffer tremendously in divorces — that most people are willing to admit. Then the next step is to convince them that their children are the foremost reason for their marriage to last, and that marriage and family is hard, practical work — not an institution based on feelings.

In a political perspective, we know that stable families are absolutely key to the survival of society: who will raise your children unless you do it? In my view, the most pressing political task in Europe is to redress the imbalances regarding the family: States should not have a "value neutral" view of this, but say clearly that marriage is preferable to cohabitation, and that divorces are sad tragedies rather than normal practice. Once this is spelt out, States should support their views in economic terms. There are relatively few politicians who dare to be clear about this today because it is more politically correct to say that "lifestyle" issues are private concerns. This may very well be; but what is a *public* issue is the conditions for raising children. Hence the public importance of the stable family.

My fourth issue in politics is *non-interference*. This may seem a really non-political issue, and perhaps it once was. Now, however, we have to restate the definitions of human rights instruments that define the freedom of religion and make sure that there remain non-political spheres in society. Freedom of religion means that Church teaching sometimes conflicts with public opinion and majority views in democracy. The right to deviate from public opinion must be ensured in practice, as it is in theory. Otherwise, majority views turn into tyranny of the majority.

Likewise, we must remind ourselves that there are non-political spheres of life and of society. This includes civil society, family and Churches. The temptation to politicise these spheres is always there. I regard this as a key area where Christians must act. Democracy is constrained by human rights, as argued above, and a major human right is the right to religious freedom. That implies the right to convert, to proselytise, to public worship, to choosing the religious education of your children, etc. It is easy to discover that these rights clash with the common views of Western society. Nonetheless it is very important to remind these very same societies of the large areas of freedom that they have to respect and not interfere with, even if the majority so wants. I could mention any number of cases where modern democracy dislikes Church teaching and would like to suppress it. But that is beyond the remit of democracy.

In sum, democracy is never better than the people that make it up. A democracy without common values that respect human dignity degenerates into tyranny. The formal requirement of rule of law and human rights are essential to democracy, which in and of itself is only a procedure if the essential equal dignity of all its members is not respected. In this chapter I have argued that the human rights approach, presented in the context of international human rights standards, is a major strategy for countering the tendency to tyranny of the majority that we observe in modern Western democracy.

June 2002

THE CHURCH'S SOCIAL TEACHING
AND THE INTERNATIONAL LABOUR ORGANIZATION'S
"DECENT WORK" STRATEGY

Ambassador JUAN SOMAVÍA *

The bonds linking the Holy See and the International Labour Organization (ILO) with its permanent Secretariat, the International Labour Office, are very old and date back almost to the ILO's foundation. In the more recent history of these relations, Pope John Paul II spoke to the International Labour Conference on 15 June 1982. He was supposed to address the Conference a year earlier, but because of the attempt on his life his visit was postponed, and it was in the intervening period that he published his Encyclical *Laborem Exercens* on human work, to which he referred in his speech.

On 1 May 2000, the Holy Father invited me, in my capacity as Director-General of the International Labour Office, to address some 150,000 employees, workers and members of government gathered at Tor Vergata on the outskirts of Rome, on the occasion of the Jubilee of Workers. There I presented our Decent Work agenda, which represents the basic strategy underlying the ILO's current activity. In response, Pope John Paul II no time in making an appeal for a worldwide coalition on behalf of Decent Work. I would therefore like to make a comparison here between this concept and the social teaching of the Catholic Church.

We shall proceed in three stages. First, we shall consider briefly the concept of decent work, as understood by the ILO and as the term is used particularly in the report which I presented and which was adopted at the 89th International Labour Conference in July 2001. Our starting point is the hopes of modern men and women. What do they expect from their work? What do they hope for in life? The decent work strategy is based on these aspirations. It involves four goals which we shall list in our attempt to arrive at an in-depth understanding of how this strategy is rooted in a number of different values.

At this level, we shall be in a position to trace the intimate connections between some of these key values and certain affirmations made in the Social Doctrine of the Catholic Church. To this end, our attention will be focused

---

* Director-General of the International Labour Office, Geneva.

principally on the Encyclical *Laborem Exercens* of 14 September 1981, while also considering some valuable elements of the Encyclical *Centesimus Annus* of 1 May 1991. We shall find here the objective and subjective dimensions of work, the priority to be given to labour in relationship to capital, and lastly the notion of the indirect employer and the principle of subsidiarity, the latter of which finds a striking application in the tripartite system used at every level of activity within the ILO.

Finally, in the concluding section, we shall endeavour to look at prospects for the future. If decent work is to become the driving force behind an Organization with a worldwide outlook, it is indispensable that it be capable of establishing its legitimacy based not only on the ethical and moral values contained in the positions of the Catholic Church but also on those found in the great traditions on which the majority of world cultures are based. It is in this regard that it will be appropriate to mention a new step taken in this sense by the convocation, within the International Labour Office, of a meeting of different traditions on the subject of the religious, spiritual and humanist values which underlie our decent work agenda. We shall be able to discern certain convergences which have come to light between the different traditions represented.

But before delving into this brief study, I wish to emphasize that I believe it essential that the modern world take note of the importance of ethical and spiritual values and references. And this must be done within the contexts of international politics, of maintaining peace and security, of human rights, of economic globalization with its social dimensions, of the equitable distribution of wealth and the fight against poverty, of the protection of the environment and of sustainable development on a planetary scale. On a personal level, confirmed by the exercise of my role as Director-General of the International Labour Office, I am profoundly convinced that the great religious, spiritual and humanist traditions with their insistence on the identity and dignity of the human person must occupy a central position in the quest for a globalization that makes sense. This explains the importance of the connection to be fostered between, on the one hand, the world or the international political system and, on the other, the different spiritual and religious traditions and what they propose in terms of the values and aspirations of the men and women of today.

This connection was made evident to all at the time of the preparation for the World Summit on Social Development. Before this Summit, the spiritual dimension of issues such as the environment, human rights, social questions, urban problems, etc. was quite simply not on the international agenda. In emphasizing the importance of work as a solution, there is no question that this Summit has essentially taken up the questions of poverty, marginalization and unemployment from the perspective of their material implications, but an opening was also clearly made to the spiritual dimension, particularly by means of questions such as "Why does work occupy a central position within every society?", or "How does the elimination of poverty and marginalization determine the moral quality of a society?". A certain number of approaches were outlined in the final text allowing the insertion of this more spiritual dimension within the international system.

Our hope here is to see how these spiritual dimensions and values can be linked to the activity of the ILO in its decent work strategy. Whence the importance of our starting point: obtaining better work under better conditions is at the heart of people's needs and expectations, on city streets as well as in the countryside, and represents a key factor in giving meaning to the reality of their daily lives.

The ILO's Decent Work Strategy

The concept of "work", as understood by the ILO's strategy, not only includes work in its contractual form within the context of organized economies, but extends also to the informal sector and to every kind of work. "It includes wage employment, self-employment and home working. It also includes the range of activities in the informal economy and the care economy".[69] This is in full accord with the definition presented at the beginning of the Encyclical *Laborem Exercens*: "Work means any activity by man, whether manual or intellectual, whatever its nature or circumstances; it means any human activity that can and must be recognized as work, in the midst of all the many activities of which man is capable and to which he is predisposed by his very nature, by virtue of humanity itself".[70]

But what do people expect? What do they hope for from their work? This is where the qualification "decent", referring to the idea of "decency", comes into play. Decency is the embodiment of human "dignity" in a particular society at a particular time in history. This word draws our attention to the fact that the concrete fulfillment of the dignity of the human person is largely dependent on local cultures and on scales of values that evolve in the history of a community. What is considered "decent" is conditioned by

---

[69] Reducing the Decent Work Deficit: A Global Challenge, Report of the Director-General to the International Labour Conference, 89th Session 2001, International Labour Office, Geneva 2001, p. 5.

[70] *Laborem Exercens*, Prologue.

culture, geography and history. This notion is found in every culture and its content can be expressed in many different ways.

If the concept of work is not to amount merely to the set of "means of sustaining life and of meeting basic needs" but is to include "also the activity through which individuals affirm their own identity, both to themselves and to those around them",[71] then it is perfectly normal for people to aspire to decent work in a stable environment. The notion of "decency" is closely connected to very personal concrete aspirations which can vary from "your job and future prospects [to] your working conditions, [to] balancing work and family life, putting your kids through school... [Decent work] is about gender equality, equal recognition... It is about having a voice in your workplace, about receiving a fair share of wealth, about developing your entrepreneurial skills... And everywhere, and for everybody, decent work is about securing human dignity".[72]

Understood in this way, the concept of decent work is not limited to a mere material dimension; it also includes a properly spiritual dimension of work. It is therefore not sufficient that employment produce income, employment must take on a certain quality. This is how each society is to pursue a decent work agenda. In effect, if it is preferable for someone to have a job rather than not to have one, and if — from this person's point of view — it is more decent to move from being unemployed to being employed, then it is nonetheless important, according to the ILO's perspective of decent work, that this employment should be made better, more decent.

In attempting to make reality correspond to all these human aspirations, we are made aware of a clear global decent work deficit. In my report to the 89th International Labour Conference, I expressed this awareness under the form of four deficits:

– the deficit of workers' rights or the denial of rights at work;
– the deficit of employment or the absence of sufficient employment opportunities;
– the deficit of social protection or inadequate social protection;
– the deficit of social dialogue or shortcomings in social dialogue.[73]

Concretely, the decent work strategy seeks first of all the universal application of the ILO Declaration of 1998 concerning the fundamental prin-

---

[71] Reducing the Decent Work Deficit: A Global Challenge, Report of the Director-General to the International Labour Conference, 89th Session 2001, pp. 5-6.

[72] Reducing the Decent Work Deficit: A Global Challenge, Report of the Director-General to the International Labour Conference, 89th Session 2001, pp. 7-8.

[73] Ibid., p. 8.

ciples and rights at work, which represent the ground or the material basis for what is decent. But this strategy seeks to bring about, beyond this basic level and without any visible upper limit, more decent working conditions for every particular situation. In summary, we can formulate four strategic goals:

– promoting and seeing to the application of norms for work, as well as the principles and rights fundamental to work, as these are contained in the 1998 ILO Declaration; [74]
– increasing the opportunities for women and men to obtain decent employment;
– expanding the benefits and effectiveness of social protection for all;
– strengthening the tripartite system and social dialogue.

By this decent work strategy the ILO fully accepts its responsibility to promote the universal dignity of human work at the international level. It does this while at the same time respecting the principle of subsidiarity, by recognizing the rights and duties of each local community, helping them to accept their responsibilities concerning the attainment of the four goals, strategic and complementary, of the decent work agenda.

It has been my desire in this brief overview to underline the decision made by the ILO to include the dimensions of value and decency in its approach to the question of work. Work involves employment and a salary, of course, but it becomes Decent Work when the worker is able to earn an honest wage and has the necessary resources to lead a stable family life, to educate his children, to grow humanly, morally, physically and spiritually; or yet again, when the worker's dignity is respected in his surroundings, in the workplace, in the society of which he is a part. Moreover, the four strategic goals of decent work readily present people's concerns and aspirations with regard to work. It is precisely in this sense that they constitute the origin, the logic and the final result of the decent work agenda, and this is basically due to the fact that the aspiration of every human being for a decent life and a better life is written in the very heart of the ILO's mandate. [75]

---

[74] This Declaration reaffirms the commitment of the international community "to respect, to promote and to realize, in good faith", freedom of association and effective recognition of workers' and employers' right to collective bargaining. States are committed also to working for the elimination of all forms of forced or compulsory labour, for the effective abolition of child labour and the elimination of discrimination in respect of employment and occupation.

[75] On 10 May 1944 the ILO strengthened its foundation in adopting the Philadelphia Declaration, which appears now as an annex to its Constitution: "Believing that experience has fully demonstrated the truth of the statement in the Constitution of the International Labour

The convergences between the ILO's Decent Work Strategy and the Social Teaching of the Catholic Church

Our attention just now was focused on the values underlying the concept of decent work, values such as human dignity, what people aspire for in life, decency, but also family, society, etc. The market economy (consumption, profit, cost, interest, capital, market, growth, etc.) does not appear to convey these values in any particular way. It is at this level of values that we find a convergence between the ILO's decent work strategy and the Church's social teaching. Three key elements from the Encyclicals *Laborem Exercens* of 14 September 1981 and *Centesimus Annus* of 1 May 1991 have caught my attention, and I would like to show how each of these strikes a strong chord in the decent work strategy. The first point is the distinction between the objective and the subjective dimensions of work; the second lies in the priority of labour in relation to capital; and the third point concerns the notion of the indirect employer joined to that of the tripartite system and subsidiarity.

The objective and subjective dimensions of work

The principal perspective of the Encyclical *Laborem Exercens* is found in the mission given to human beings: "Be fruitful and multiply, and fill the earth and subdue it".[76] Even if this verse does not refer directly or explicitly to work, it certainly makes an indirect allusion to work as an activity to be undertaken in the world by human beings. Moreover, does not the second account of Creation in the Book of Genesis put the natural element of water on the same level as work, as jointly necessary for the development of the earth?[77] These words show thus the deepest essence of work. It is a "transitive" activity, that is to say, its source is found in the human subject, its aim is to produce an external object destined for other human persons. It presupposes a specific quality of human beings over every other element of the earth and, in turn, it confirms and develops this specific quality: that of being a person destined to enter into relationship with other persons. In this Chris-

---

Organization that lasting peace can be established only if it is based on social justice, the Conference affirms that: all human beings, irrespective of race, creed or sex, have the right to pursue both their material well-being *and their spiritual development* [emphasis added by the author of this article] in conditions of freedom and dignity, of economic security and equal opportunity". Cf. http://ilo.org/public/english/iloconst.htm#annex.

[76] *Gen* 1:28.

[77] "In the day that the Lord God made the earth and the heavens, when no plant of the field was yet in the earth and no herb of the field had yet sprung up – for the Lord God had not caused it to rain upon the earth, and there was no man to till the ground": *Gen* 2:4-5.

tian conception, human beings were created not as lone creatures but, from the very beginning, as relational beings, "man and woman", "in the image of God". The mission given to them from the very beginning, to be creators in their own turn, is universal and concerns all human beings, every generation, every phase of economic and cultural development. Each and every person, in the measure appropriate to each one and in a countless number of ways, participates in this immense process by which human beings "subdue the earth through their work".[78]

From this it follows first of all that human beings are involved as *subjects* in the work process and, second, that this process itself is trans-generational insofar as the present generation inherits from the past the open-ended opportunities concerning work and that the coming generation will inherit from us a number of increasing opportunities. It is at this stage that the difference between the objective and subjective dimensions of work appears.

The *objective* dimension itself surpasses every end result of a particular work. It goes beyond the objects produced and the services rendered by work and consumed in the present. The principal objective result of work for the coming generation is the *technology* that progressively emerges from each type of work insofar as it is human capital in growth. It is true that certain types of work are more oriented to consumption by the present generation while others — research, for example — are more oriented to the growth of technology. But, in the final analysis, everyone uses and contributes to technology, even if only partially or slightly. Nonetheless, if this technology improves the quantity and quality of objects produced by work, it can also be transformed from being an ally of human beings to becoming a quasi-adversary, for example, when the mechanization of work "supplants" human beings, taking away all their personal satisfaction, all their creativity and responsibility. The extolling of machines can lead to reducing human beings to the status of being slaves to machines.[79]

The Encyclical *Laborem Exercens* then presents the *subjective* dimension of work: "work in the subjective sense: man as the subject of work". This section insists on the idea that men and women, insofar as they are "the image of God", are human persons; that is to say, man is "a subjective being capable of acting in a planned and rational way, capable of deciding about himself, and with a tendency to self-realization. As a person, man is therefore the subject of work... he performs various actions belonging to the work process; independently of their objective content, these actions must all serve

[78] *Laborem Exercens*, 4.
[79] *Laborem Exercens*, 5.

90

to realize his humanity, to fulfill the calling to be a person that is his by reason of his very humanity".[80] Each of us has clear experience of what this means. In effect, are we not in our inner-most being affected by our work, through the recognition and the respect that we receive from others, through the relationships that we establish at work? It is evidently very important that we fulfill ourselves as human beings. Whether someone is CEO of a multi-national company, secretary, lab researcher, bricklayer or even a religious leading a contemplative life, all of us are deeply shaped by our life of work, even if the objective dimension of our work, in other words, what we produce, is very different.

The social teaching of the Catholic Church insists on the fundamental ethical fact that "work is a good thing for man... It is not only good in the sense that it is useful or something to enjoy; it is also good as being something worthy, that is to say, something that corresponds to man's dignity, that expresses this dignity and increases it... Through work man not only transforms nature, adapting it to his own needs, but he also achieves fulfillment as a human being and indeed, in a sense, becomes 'more a human being'... All this pleads in favour of the moral obligation to link industriousness as a virtue with the social order of work, which will enable man to become, in work, 'more a human being' and not be degraded by it... especially through damage to the dignity and subjectivity that are proper to him".[81]

This dignity and this subjectivity of the worker are not merely private or personal matters but also involve the person as a member of a family and a nation. As far as the family is concerned, the Encyclicals *Laborem Exercens* and *Centesimus Annus* affirm: "Work constitutes a foundation for the formation of family life... In a way, work is a condition for making it possible to found a family, since the family requires the means of subsistence which man normally gains through work. Work and industriousness also influence the whole process of education in the family, for the very reason that everyone 'becomes a human being' through, among other things, work, and becoming a human being is precisely the main purpose of the whole process of education. Obviously, two aspects of work in a sense come into play here: the one making family life and its upkeep possible, and the other making possible the achievement of the purposes of the family, especially education".[82]

---

[80] *Laborem Exercens*, 6.
[81] *Laborem Exercens*, 9.
[82] *Laborem Exercens*, 10.

I was very pleased to note that the Encyclical *Laborem Exercens* emphasizes a point that is very much present at the very heart of the ILO's mandate: the struggle against the tendency to increase the importance of the objective dimension of work and to relegate the subjective dimension to a secondary level, which represents a threat to the true hierarchy of values. In "various trends of materialistic and economistic thought ... work was understood and treated as a sort of 'merchandise' that the worker — especially the industrial worker — sells to the employer, who at the same time is the possessor of the capital, that is to say, of all the working tools and means that make production possible... [It is] a one-sidedly materialistic civilization which gives prime importance to the objective dimension of work, while the subjective dimension — everything in direct or indirect relationship with the subject of work — remains on a secondary level".[83] In order to counteract this threat, it is absolutely necessary for workers to be organized. In this context, the Church since the nineteenth century has forcefully supported this movement of "solidarity between workers", particularly in the first Encyclical dealing with work, *Rerum Novarum*, published in 1891 by Pope Leo XIII. "In order to achieve social justice in the various parts of the world, in the various countries, and in the relationships between them, there is a need for ever new movements of solidarity of the workers and with the workers".[84] The Church is resolutely committed to this cause because she considers it part of her mission, indeed as a test of her fidelity to the Gospel. The Encyclicals *Laborem Exercens* and *Centesimus Annus* insist on the role played by unions in protecting the vital interests of workers, which include "work and personal dignity".

These different concepts developed by the Encyclical *Laborem Exercens* and taken up anew in the Encyclical *Centesimus Annus* are in complete accord with the ILO's general understanding of the concept of "work". I stressed this in my report to the 89th Session of the International Labour Conference in 2001, entitled *Reducing the Decent Work Deficit: A Global Challenge*.

The 1944 Philadelphia Declaration, redefining the goals of the ILO, affirms that "labour is not a commodity". And even if the "labour market" determines the price of labour, it must never be forgotten that part of the cost of production turns out in the end to be a human person. An employer pays for "something" that before anything else is "someone". This is a basic

---

[83] *Laborem Exercens*, 7.
[84] *Laborem Exercens*, 8.

ethical value for the ILO, which is convinced that the person in the midst of society must never be defined by the market.

Moreover, work is not merely "the means of sustaining life... but it is also the activity through which individuals affirm their own identity... Everybody seeks a fair chance to prosper in life by their own endeavours".[85] Once again, the 1944 Philadelphia Declaration stipulates that the ILO aims at achieving "the employment of workers in the occupations in which they can have the satisfaction of giving the fullest measure of their skill and attainments and make their greatest contribution to the common well-being", and that "all human beings... have the right to pursue both their material well-being and their spiritual development in conditions of freedom and dignity". It is clear that in its very foundation decent work concerns the right of everyone to develop himself "in conditions of freedom and dignity, of economic security and equal opportunity".[86] As we have already emphasized, "everywhere, and for everybody, decent work is about securing human dignity".[87]

More specifically, the first goal of the decent work strategy, the promotion of the 1998 ILO Declaration on fundamental principles and rights at work, embodies entirely the subjective dimension of work. In work, it is men and women who, as individual persons making up an anonymous work force, are most important. We have already seen that the Encyclical *Laborem Exercens* proceeds in exactly this same sense. But here, we can refer to the connection established by this Encyclical between the positive appreciation of work ("work is... something good, and so man develops through love for work") and human rights. "This entirely positive and creative, educational and meritorious character of man's work must be the basis for the judgments and decisions being made today in its regard in spheres that include human rights".[88] The Catholic Church's social teaching makes reference to international declarations on work and more specifically to the ILO as "one organization fostering such initiatives on the international level".[89] Let us take a

---

[85] Reducing the Decent Work Deficit: A Global Challenge, Report of the Director-General to the International Labour Conference, 89th Session 2001, pp. 5-6.

[86] Reducing the Decent Work Deficit: A Global Challenge, Report of the Director-General to the International Labour Conference, 89th Session, 2001, p. 7.

[87] Reducing the Decent Work Deficit: A Global Challenge, Report of the Director-General to the International Labour Conference, 89th Session 2001, p. 8.

[88] *Laborem Exercens*, 11.

[89] *Laborem Exercens*, 11. We do well to emphasize here that it was Albert Thomas, the first Director-General of the International Labour Office, who in 1920 discovered the importance of social Catholicism and decided to strengthen the ILO's relationship with the Catholic Church. After five years of negotiations, it was understood that the Holy See

closer look at the four components of the ILO Declaration on fundamental principles and rights at work, adopted by the International Labour Conference at its 86th session in Geneva on 18 June 1998 (known later on as the 1998 Declaration).

The elimination of forced labour represents the fundamental recognition of the subjective dimension of work. If our only concern is the objective dimension of work, the least costly way to get a job done is probably forced labour. If the ILO proposes the elimination of forced labour as one of the fundamental rights at work, it does so precisely because of the inalienable value of the human being as an individual. A person must never and can never be absorbed into a simple work force, like a robot that functions 24 hours a day. This aspect is inscribed in the 1919 ILO Constitution and in the 1944 Philadelphia Declaration, in the statement that "labour is not a commodity".

The elimination of any kind of discrimination in respect of employment and occupation according to "race, colour, sex, religion, political opinion, national extraction or social origin",[90] clearly means that, following these criteria, every person is to be considered in an equal manner, with the same respect, and that the person is never an isolated individual but the result of a complex network of individuals connected among themselves and attaining in this way his or her human personality in the context of families and nations.

The abolition of child labour clearly insists on the importance of the family in which children have the possibility to grow and develop their abilities fully for the good of the future of humanity.[91] They are to be considered persons with their own rights who are to be protected from their earliest years.[92] The ILO is moreover very much aware of the social connection between personal dignity and the family. Work is a fundamental component of family stability. It is quite evident that the income and the satisfaction derived from work have a direct impact on family life and on the quality

would propose three candidates, from among whom the Director-General of the International Labour Office would choose a special counselor, who would become a functionary of the International Labour Organization. The Holy See has always asked the Society of Jesus (the Jesuits) to find the candidates for this office. After the Reverend Fathers André Arnou (1926-1933), Achille Danset (1934-1935), Albert Le Roy (1936-1955), Joseph Joblin (1955-1981), John Lucal (1981-1986) and Louis Christiaens (1987-1996), it is currently the Reverend Father Dominique Peccoud who, since 1996, has occupied this post.

[90] ILO Convention No. 111, on Discrimination (Employment and Occupation), of 1958.

[91] This was the goal of the ILO Convention No. 138, on the Minimum Age for Workers.

[92] The ILO Convention No. 182, on the elimination of the worst forms of child labour, sought to protect children insofar as they are children and not as future workers.

94

of family relationships. The connection with the education of children is firmly established. "An unemployed person means a very unhappy family. Lack of work for parents breeds tension, family violence and abuse. It affects children at school, brings them closer to crime and drugs, and all too often, to child labour".[93] We can therefore conclude that decent work has major implications for a proper equilibrium between work and family life.

The last goal (and in fact the first point of the 1998 Declaration) concerns the freedom of association and the right to collective bargaining of workers and employers. This represents the recognition of the solidarity that is necessary among workers, but also among employers, in order that they can act collectively. We have already indicated that one of the areas of decent work deficit is found precisely at the level of social dialogue, known also as the "representational gap" which is explained by the fact that "workers and employers have frequently, and for diverse reasons, not organized to make their voices heard".[94]

The ILO and the social teaching of the Catholic Church are on the same track when both institutions affirm the value of work as the source of personal dignity, of family stability and peace within the community. If work is first of all connected with personal development, we are convinced — together with the Church — that work also has a stabilizing and educational value in the family and builds well-being and harmony within nations and between them.[95] It is true that this new "actor", which is the Market, is important, but it is and must remain at the service of the dignity and the quality of life of persons, and in general it should be a tool allowing them, through their social relations, to create well-being, stability and peace for themselves and others, within their families and in society worldwide. This is what we call "the common good"; but, very often, this formula is turned around and capital or market values tend to take the upper hand over the values of dignity, family, society and peace. This is what I wish to examine more closely in the next section.

---

[93] Reducing the Decent Work Deficit: A Global Challenge, Report of the Director-General to the International Labour Conference, 89th Session 2001, p. 6.

[94] Reducing the Decent Work Deficit: A Global Challenge, Report of the Director-General to the International Labour Conference, 89th Session 2001, p. 10.

[95] We can think here of the basic intuition of the "fathers" of the ILO, who felt the need to ensure that the peace established after the First World War would be founded on social harmony within the different nations.

The priority of labour in relation to capital

A second point of convergence between the ILO and the social teaching of the Catholic Church gravitates around the imbalance between capital and labour. The Church points out that the Industrial Revolution of the nineteenth century gave rise to a "great conflict that ... emerged between 'capital' and 'labour' " [96] and that this opposition has had repercussions in a systematic class struggle. The Encyclical *Laborem Exercens* forcefully affirms "the priority of labour over capital. This principle directly concerns the process of production: in this process labour is always a primary efficient cause, while capital, the whole collection of means of production, remains a mere instrument or instrumental cause".[97] Capital is described as "not only the natural resources placed at man's disposal but also the whole collection of means by which man appropriates natural resources and transforms them". However, these means remain at the same time "the result of the historical heritage of human labour". Capital is thus understood as being "everything that is at the service of work, everything that in the present state of technology constitutes its ever more highly perfected 'instrument' ", but which nonetheless remains "the result of work".[98] Capital is, in the strict sense, a collection of things, since human beings, as persons and the subject of work, have primacy over capital: "We must emphasize and give prominence to the primacy of man in the production process, the primacy of man over things".[99]

It is true that capital cannot be separated from labour, but labour is in no way placed in opposition to capital. Labour and capital are interdependent and intimately connected, because it is essentially in the workplace that workers are heirs to a twofold legacy: natural resources and the technology developed by their predecessors (in other words, capital). A rupture comes to light when labour is separated from capital and finds itself placed in opposition to capital, as though labour and capital were two impersonal forces that should necessarily be in conflict with one another. At the same time there is also a rupture in the principle of the primacy of the human person over things. The Encyclical *Laborem Exercens* forcefully condemns "the error of economism, that of considering human labour solely according to its economic purpose", as well as "an error of materialism, in that economism directly or indirectly includes a conviction of the primacy and superiority of the material, and directly or indirectly places the spiritual and the personal

---

[96] *Laborem Exercens*, 11.
[97] *Laborem Exercens*, 12.
[98] *Laborem Exercens*, 12.
[99] *Laborem Exercens*, 12.

... in a position of subordination to material reality".[100] Rapid industrialization and "primitive" or "uncontrolled" capitalism were imprisoned in a self-righteous ignorance concerning men, women and even children as human persons endowed with personal dignity.

What the Encyclical *Laborem Exercens* describes, on the contrary, as a "right labour system" is one that "in its very basis ... overcomes the opposition between labour and capital through an effort at being shaped in accordance with the principle put forward above: the principle of the substantial and real priority of labour, of the subjectivity of human labour and its effective participation in the whole production process".[101]

As far as the right to possession or to private property is concerned, the Encyclical recalls that this right is never absolute but "is subordinated to the right to common use".[102] This means that even if the Encyclical accepts the principle of private ownership of the means of production, it maintains reservations with regard to the isolation of the means of production as separated property (capital) in opposition to labour. This is seen as being "contrary to the very nature of these means and their possession. They cannot be possessed against labour".[103] They must always be placed at the disposal and at the service of labour, and in order to ensure common access to these goods, "the socialization ... of certain means of production" is legitimate.[104] Socialization clearly means that "on the basis of his work each person is fully entitled to consider himself a partowner of the great workbench at which he is working with every one else".[105] Labour then becomes associated with capital and not opposed to it, for example "joint ownership of the means of work, sharing by the workers in the management and/or profits of businesses... etc.".[106]

The Encyclical's position that capital is secondary and subordinate to the principle of the priority of labour is built on "a postulate of the order of social morality".[107] It is the worker who is primary. He is not a simple tool of production nor merchandise that can be hired and let go after he has been used; rather, he is a true subject of work who fulfills himself completely as a human being by the expedience of his work. Human aspirations are not

---

[100] *Laborem Exercens*, 13.
[101] *Laborem Exercens*, 13.
[102] *Laborem Exercens*, 14.
[103] *Laborem Exercens*, 14.
[104] *Laborem Exercens*, 14.
[105] *Laborem Exercens*, 14.
[106] *Laborem Exercens*, 14.
[107] *Laborem Exercens*, 15.

exhausted in the sphere of economics, they are, before anything else, personal values. Moreover, the economic system itself benefits when these personal values are taken fully into consideration. This includes the possibility that "the human person can preserve his awareness of working 'for himself' ".[108]

This conviction of the necessity of considering labour and capital together can be found once again not only in the ILO's insistence on the dignity of the worker but also in the second dimension of the ILO's strategy concerning decent work. This seeks to increase the possibilities for men and women to find decent employment. In pursuing this goal, the ILO considers the capitalist undertaking merely as one way among others for creating employment. A sustained effort is made to create and support small and medium-sized businesses. In effect, they create the majority of employment offers. Regarding the merging of existing companies into large multinationals, this must not occur by taking into account only considerations of capital and suppressing too large a number of jobs, and it must also promote permanent formation and credit policies that ensure that the salaried employees can find work in other sectors within the new structure. In this way, the expansion of independent employment through micro-credit and the development of cooperatives represent two parallel quests for the ILO. For this, the priority is the creation of jobs, since work is the best means for helping people to escape poverty and to become more human. These efforts respond to the appeal made in the Encyclical *Laborem Exercens* to "act against unemployment, which in all cases is an evil, and which, when it reaches a certain level, can become a real social disaster".[109]

The ILO's strategy aimed at reducing the lack of employment does not strive to strengthen capital but rather to develop employment for every person; capital is only one of many factors that can contribute to this end. In the ILO's understanding, development is defined as the expansion of people's capabilities, and hence of their freedoms.[110] Here once more we find the same principle of the priority of the human being and of labour over capital. The purpose of the decent work strategy is workers' dignity, family stability and social harmony; the success of a capitalistic economic system is one important means among others for attaining this end. The ILO has always maintained that the fundamental principles and rights that it defends have no need of justification. "Achieving fundamental rights is not only a

---

[108] *Laborem Exercens*, 15.

[109] *Laborem Exercens*, 18.

[110] Cf. Reducing the Decent Work Deficit: A Global Challenge, Report of the Director-General to the International Labour Conference, 89th Session 2001, p. 26.

goal in itself, it is also a critical determinant of the capabilities of people to realize their aspirations".[111]

The attainment of workers' rights is never, however, the simple consequence of an economic system guided by the principle of maximum profit. This agrees with what the Encyclical *Laborem Exercens* states: "On the contrary, it is respect for the objective rights of the worker... that must constitute the adequate and fundamental criterion for shaping the whole economy".[112] The Encyclical moreover makes reference to the ILO's contributions in the area of establishing a policy on work that is ethically correct. This point is echoed in the third aspect of ILO's strategy: that of reducing the deficit of social protection. When the ILO gets involved in programmes aimed at increasing work security and at promoting social security systems, its desire above all is to highlight the fact that there can be no decent work without a minimum of work security. "... basic security for all in different development contexts is fundamental for both social justice and economic dynamism and is essential if people are to function to the best of their capabilities".[113]

This approach argues that rights and economic progress go hand in hand. An economy's success is often measured by the rate of growth in production or revenue, whereas social progress is linked to the exercise of certain rights and freedoms, to security, to social protection. There is no opposition between economic growth and social progress: "work undertaken in decent conditions and for a decent income can also contribute to economic efficiency".[114] For the ILO, "decent work is a goal in its own right, but it can also have a positive effect on productivity and economic growth. Neither productivity nor social justice are 'dirty words' for the ILO. On the contrary, they can be successfully combined".[115] Decent work can very well be productive and profitable! To give an illustration, I refer to the WISE method (Work Improvement in Small Enterprises) which was fine-tuned by the International Labour Office to improve the working conditions and productivity of small businesses.[116] This strategy reflects well the tenor of the En-

---

[111] Reducing the Decent Work Deficit: A Global Challenge, Report of the Director-General to the International Labour Conference, 89th Session 2001, p. 27.

[112] *Laborem Exercens*, 17.

[113] Reducing the Decent Work Deficit: A Global Challenge, Report of the Director-General to the International Labour Conference, 89th Session 2001, p. 10.

[114] Reducing the Decent Work Deficit: A Global Challenge, Report of the Director-General to the International Labour Conference, 89th Session 2001, p. 20.

[115] *Ibid.*

[116] The seventh survey of the follow-up given to the Tripartite Declaration of Principles concerning Multinational Enterprises and Social Policy, undertaken by the ILO in 2000, brought together many examples that show how important it is to foster the bonds

cyclical *Laborem Exercens* by its refusal to be lulled into an opposition of or a separation between, on the one hand, workers/social progress and, on the other, capital/profits/economic growth.

The principle of indirect employer and subsidiarity in the tripartite system of the ILO

The third point of convergence between the ILO strategy and the social teaching of the Catholic Church is found at the level of social dialogue, in which the principles of subsidiarity, indirect employment and the ILO's tripartite system enter into play.

An *indirect employer* is defined in the Encyclical as persons or institutions that determine the whole complex of the socio-economic system, which itself arises from collective work contracts and from the principles of conduct established by these persons or institutions. Such employers include all organizations working on the national level (the State, social institutions, etc.), the regional level (the European Union, NAFTA, MERCOSUR, the Association of South East Asian Nations, etc.), and the international level (multilateral organizations such as the ILO, the Food and Agriculture Organization of the UN, the World Bank, etc.) [117] that are responsible for the global orientation of work policies. "The indirect employer substantially determines one or other facet of the labour relationship, thus conditioning the conduct of the direct employer when the latter determines in concrete terms the actual work contract and labour relations".[118] There is, then, a whole network of influences that condition the conduct of indirect employers.

The final aspect of the ILO's decent work strategy, which seeks to reduce the deficit of social dialogue, promotes the role of the indirect employer, and does so in the perspective of strengthening social partners and their dialogue concerning the goals of decent work. This is all the more urgent when we consider that the ever-increasing gap between rich and poor produces "an effect on local labour policy and on the worker's situation in the economi-

---

with the local economy and how the improvement of competences, social policies and social dialogue contribute to economic growth. For businesses, decent work is a means for becoming more competitive. We can take the example of the Adidas company. Cf. *Reducing the Decent Work Deficit: A Global Challenge*, Report of the Director-General to the International Labour Conference, 89th Session 2001, pp. 22-25.

[117] The Encyclical *Laborem Exercens* makes explicit reference to the fact that the mutual dependence of societies and States requires international cooperation, a cooperation brought about by means of treaties and agreements. The base criterion of these pacts and conventions must likewise be that of human work as a fundamental right of every person.

[118] *Laborem Exercens*, 17.

cally disadvantaged societies [or in informal economies]. Finding himself in a system thus conditioned, the direct employer fixes working conditions below the objective requirements of the workers".[119] Can we not make a connection between the concept of *indirect employer* and the principle of *subsidiarity*, this latter against the backdrop of the tripartite system that characterizes each step of action taken by the ILO, whether local, national, regional or international? The principle of subsidiarity has been developed by the Church with regard to every hierarchical society and explains that all problems must be resolved at the hierarchical level closest to that at which they occur, without making recourse abusively to a higher level. The Encyclical *Centesimus Annus* of 1991, marking the centenary of the famous Encyclical *Rerum Novarum* of Pope Leo XIII, emphasizes the need for reforms that will protect and restore the dignity of work as a free activity of the human being. "These reforms imply that society and the State will both assume responsibility, especially for protecting the worker from the nightmare of unemployment... [for ensuring] wage levels adequate for the maintenance of the worker and his family... [for providing] careful controls and adequate legislative measures to block shameful forms of exploitation... [for guaranteeing] 'humane' working hours and adequate freetime... as well as the right to express one's own personality at the workplace".[120] In all of these examples, the negotiating role of unions in dialogue with employers is decisive. But, "the State must contribute to the achievement of these goals both directly and indirectly. Indirectly and according to the principle of subsidiarity, by creating favourable conditions for the free exercise of economic activity, which will lead to abundant opportunities for employment and sources of wealth".[121]

Thus, it is clear that public authorities, including international organizations such as the ILO, must commit themselves to promoting social progress for the benefit of all citizens. Such an intervention on the part of these public authorities — who at the same time exercise the role of indirect employers — aims at providing encouragement, stimulation, regulation and completion, and is founded on the principle of subsidiarity. This principle implies first of all that individuals should be authorized to act and to speak, either for themselves or for others, in order to defend in one way or another their interests, for example, through a process of tripartite dialogue by unions and employer associations.

[119] *Laborem Exercens*, 17.
[120] *Centesimus Annus*, 15. We can easily recognize here the four pillars of the decent work strategy.
[121] *Centesimus Annus*, 15.

It seems that a certain convergence can thus be seen between the social teaching of the Catholic Church and the activity of the ILO. This convergence is found in the conviction that governments, labour organizations and employer organizations must be encouraged to plan a future that is in keeping with the dignity of each person who works. The ILO is guided by an ethic of encouragement, inspiration and motivation at every level in order to promote the actuation of norms or regulations, without seeking to impose, order or dictate by force. It is in this sense, then, that the ILO is truly an indirect employer. Instead of imposing its conventions and recommendations all at once upon its members, it insists in its decent work strategy on four types of fundamental conventions which, if universally put into practice, would signal the beginning of a process of gradual adoption of other juridical instruments. We have already seen that it is a question here of everything connected with the Freedom of Association, with Forced Labour, with Child Labour and with Discrimination.[122] This ethic of motivation and not repression reflects the ILO's ambition to bring about profound, long-term social progress in human communities.

The ILO's ethic of activity concentrates its efforts on many "hierarchical" levels: local, national, regional and international. In order that the different instruments of the ILO be applied effectively, it is important that none of these levels should be short-circuited or neglected. This is in perfect agreement with the principle of subsidiarity, which rightly rejects any kind of "parachuting" of solutions or regulations from any level higher than that where the problem to be resolved arises. I wish to show how the principle of subsidiarity, so dear to the Church, comes into play at each of the different levels of activity of the ILO: the international level of drafting international conventions and recommendations, the national level of ratifying these, and the level of applying them to businesses (including the procedures to be followed); and all this is done without neglecting or minimizing any of these levels.

At the international level of drafting and adoption, the instruments of the ILO are worked out over a long period of time, with many years of tripartite international discussion led by the International Labour Office to fine-tune texts proposed successively so that matters of national concern may be clearly distinguished from problems of a worldwide import. It is then possible to propose a text that will be discussed by the tripartite delegations of all the member States which wish to take part; this is done in the commis-

---

[122] Conventions Nos. 29 and 105, on forced labour; Conventions Nos. 87 and 98, on the freedom of association; Conventions Nos. 100 and 111, on discrimination; Conventions Nos. 138 and 182, on child labour.

sions of the two successive International Labour Conferences, before the final adoption in the plenary assembly. The Encyclical *Laborem Exercens* suggests exactly the same thing when it refers to "the mutual dependence of societies and States and the need to collaborate in various areas", explaining further that, "while preserving the sovereign rights of each society and State in the field of planning and organizing labour in its own society, action in this important area must also be taken in the dimension of international collaboration by means of the necessary treaties and agreements".[123]

At the national level of ratification, the instruments adopted are not legislative texts subject to an immediate universal application. They constitute rules that are meant to be used as reference points for local norms, in the same way that the rules of grammar of a language are used to construct correct sentences that can be understood in the particular context where they are spoken. When a State decides to ratify a convention adopted by the ILO, this convention does not for that reason become immediately applicable. For this to happen, steps must be taken at the national level to introduce, adapt or even transpose the said convention into the national juridical order, taking into consideration the socio-economic context of the country in question. The Constitution of the ILO (article 19 §3) establishes that certain climatic conditions, the imperfect development of industrial organization, or other special circumstances can be taken into consideration by the International Labour Conference in order to suggest modifications to the conventions or recommendations. The International Labour Office is moreover always at the disposition of governments to assist or guide them in this work of transposition.[124]

The transposition of the ILO norms involves a reformulation in the existing national legislation. This is done by tripartite discussions in democratic debate on the social implications of putting the said convention or recommendation into effect. When subsidiarity is put into practice in this way, it becomes possible to avert a form of emerging globalization on a worldwide scale based on only one vision and giving rise to only one way of acting. If we desire a lasting globalization, it becomes ever more important

---

[123] *Laborem Exercens*, 18.

[124] A well-known example is the ILO's IPEC programme, which seeks to reduce child labour in connection with Convention No. 182, on the Elimination of worst forms of child labour. This programme is currently being implemented in a hundred countries. For example, in Romania the IPEC programme has trained 25 work inspectors as well as five members of the Child Labour Unit as instructors who, throughout the country, are in contact not only with 680 work inspectors, but also with local authorities, worker and employer agencies, the general public and children themselves. For more information, cf. The World of Work, the Magazine of the ILO, No. 41, December 2001, pp. 8, 41 and 43.

to respect this principle of subsidiarity, according to which every problem is to be debated and resolved at the same hierarchical level at which it arises. It is for this reason that I believe that the ILO subscribes very strongly to the principle of subsidiarity.[125] At the national level, this means that globalization cannot give rise to the discarding of the socio-economic context of a particular State. Thus, no level can be neglected or discarded, but this position requires consequently that qualified representatives must be available at every level, international, national, regional and local. This is equally important at the level of businesses themselves.

At the level of concrete application in businesses, it is clear that when citizens of a country themselves take charge of their working conditions, they are in a better position than anyone else to deal with the changes taking place in the context of their work and lives. But in order to have qualified representatives at the business level, the freedom of association is a condition *sine qua non* for people to make their voices and social demands heard.

The ILO has always stressed the importance of the freedom of association and of collective negotiation as an obligation for every member of the ILO, well before the 1998 Declaration. The Encyclical *Laborem Exercens* likewise emphasizes the right of association and the role of unions, seeing them as indispensable components of social life and "a mouthpiece for the struggle for social justice, for the just rights of working people".[126] In the context of the principle of subsidiarity, the Church recognizes the importance of unions as "a constructive factor of social order and solidarity".[127]

When multinational companies are the principle actors, the risk is present that the national level with its specific socio-economic context — including the base level of the company — will be made irrelevant. It is necessary, then, that multilateral government structures together with unions ensure that international regulations and conflict resolution are respected. Much has already been accomplished but much remains to be done. I am referring here to the "Tripartite Declaration of Principles concerning Multinational Enterprises and Social Policy", adopted in 1974 by governments, labour associations and employer organizations, and re-affirmed again in 2001. That this level of application must not be underestimated is shown by the great number of volunteer and private initiatives that have arisen in recent

---

[125] This is implicitly contained in the fourth clause of the Preamble of the 1998 Declaration, saying that it is necessary to "mobilize and encourage international, regional and national efforts".

[126] *Laborem Exercens*, 20.

[127] *Laborem Exercens*, 20.

years, which, although they do not have the force of law, serve to improve and complete the situation regulated by the law.

One final thing I wish to stress is that the tripartite system is fully present at each of these "hierarchical" levels of action in the sense that none of the three constituent parties (governments, workers and employers) are excluded and that the final result of every effort at each level is inspired by continuous dialogue between the three constituent parties. This tripartite system is considered the driving force behind the potential social progress of every society, that which permits at the same time that progress is rooted in a specific socio-economic context. It is therefore no surprise that the tripartite system at each level — local, national, regional and international — is part of the historical mandate of the ILO in the area of labour rights, of social dialogue and of social protection. The role of this tripartite system is always to promote and animate (or re-animate) social dialogue at every level of action, as well as at the international level of drawing up international conventions and recommendations, at the national level of ratification and at the level of businesses.

I believe that this tripartite system can be seen as a further illustration of the principle of subsidiarity. The ILO Constitution specifies that none of the three ILO constituents — governments, workers and employers — should interfere in the sphere of another constituent, precisely in respect of the others and to avoid supplanting them. It would be contrary to the principle of subsidiarity if one of the three constituents supplanted, dominated or took the place of another constituent. This would be the case, for example, if a government undermined the base level of workers of a company, by taking their place and taking it upon itself to defend their interests under the pretext of greater effectiveness, thereby reducing them to silence. Is not this the very situation that the Church criticizes when she speaks of the "welfare State"? The Encyclical *Centesimus Annus* states it unambiguously: "excesses and abuses, especially in recent years, have provoked very harsh criticisms of the Welfare State, dubbed the 'Social Assistance State'. Malfunctions and defects in the Social Assistance State are the result of an inadequate understanding of the tasks proper to the State. Here again the principle of subsidiarity must be respected: a community of a higher order should not interfere in the internal life of a community of a lower order, depriving the latter of its functions, but rather should support it in case of need... By intervening directly and depriving society of its responsibility, the Social Assistance State leads to a loss of human energies and an inordinate increase of public agencies... In fact, it would appear that needs are best understood and satisfied by people who are closest to them and who act as neighbours to those in need".[128]

We must also recognize that beyond the activity of governments and unions on the national and international level, new institutions and new patterns of behaviour have emerged as a supplemental level seeking to firmly incorporate certain social values in the global economy. Ethical considerations have an increasing impact on the economic activity of firms, consumers and investors. Consumers, especially those from Western countries, are willing to pay more for goods produced in decent conditions, and groups arising within civil society strive to promote equality between men and women, protection of the environment and respect for human rights in global production chains. Let us take the example of the 1998 Declaration: more and more often its principles are included in codes of ethics adopted by private businesses and investment funds as well as in international agreements.[129]

All of this shows, I believe, a strong convergence between the principle of subsidiarity and the tripartite system of the ILO as it works at its three levels, the international level of drawing up ILO conventions and recommendations, the national level of ratification and transposition of international instruments in national socio-economic contexts, and lastly the level of businesses in the area of applying and following the adopted norms.

Conclusion and perspective of interreligious openness

Our reflection has focused on the theme of values in the ILO strategy dealing with decent work. The point of departure of our strategy is that of the aspirations, the expectations of men and women in their work. We are speaking here of decent work, one that permits personal growth, family stability, peace and sustainable development in society. "Everywhere and for everyone, decent work is synonymous with human dignity". The four strategic goals of decent work seek to respond to this and thereby transmit a certain number of values: dignity of the human person, family, education, personal development, social harmony, decency, protection, dialogue, employment, etc. It is at this level of values promoted by the ILO that we have found convergences with the values espoused by the social teaching of the Catholic Church, more specifically in John Paul II's two Encyclicals *Laborem Exercens* and *Centesimus Annus*. The question here is the common under-

---

[128] *Centesimus Annus*, 48.
[129] Reducing the Decent Work Deficit: A Global Challenge, Report of the Director-General to the International Labour Conference, 89th Session 2001, p. 40.

standing that these two institutions share regarding the subjective and objective dimension of work, regarding the priority of labour over capital, and regarding the importance of the indirect employer and of subsidiarity against the backdrop of a tripartite system.

Instead of offering a "concluding summary" of what I have said, I prefer to conclude this reflection on decent work and values by broadening our perspective of what concerns the ethical and spiritual references of the decent work strategy. This is made more than just a simple exercise of semantics by the conviction that the global system of the market economy lacks "legitimacy". For this reason it is indispensable that decent work should be supported by the ethical and moral values contained in the world's great religious and spiritual traditions. Two advantages arise from this. The universality of our decent work strategy will be reinforced if it is borne by the values found in the different religious and spiritual traditions from throughout the world. At the same time, this will permit a better local and regional acceptance or diffusion of the decent work strategy if men and women, workers, employers and governments discover in it a presence of the values of their own humanist, spiritual or religious tradition or culture.

However, I would first of all like to dwell on the fragility of globalization and its lack of "legitimacy" because of the absence of an ethical or moral foundation. The worldwide rules of the game in economic and monetary matters are established by force, domination and the power to impose them, and not on a free and democratic assent. This is the Achille's heel of the world economic system as we know it today. Like a dictatorship founded on violence and force, this system at first seems unshakable and solid, but in fact it risks being swept away sooner or later. The recent crisis in Argentina is a tragic example of this, but how many others will follow? Some of the biggest companies quoted on the stock market disappear one after another, and why? It is the lack of ethical legitimacy and the universal intrusion of corruption and lies that represent a crippling weakness of the world economic system. There is, then, an urgent need for the world economy to examine the moral values that might underlie its reconstruction. It is at this level that the ILO would like to propose goals and values on which globalization can be based.

As Director-General of the International Labour Office I was present at the Davos World Economic Forum in New York as well as at the Social Summit of Porto Alegre in Brazil, where I presented the ILO's strategy concerning decent work. We can note that in Porto Alegre, a part of the ILO constituents — under the form of national and international unions — was present at the meeting for a different globalization. If the attitude there was not that of a categorical and overwhelming rejection of globalization, it was more the neo-liberal type of globalization that became the object of criticism. The decent work strategy was received as a correction of the system, presenting possibilities for solutions to the demands which were the cause of street protests. "Everywhere and for everyone, decent work", synonymous with human dignity, could have been shouted there as a slogan. At the time of the Davos Economic Forum in New York the leaders of important multi-national enterprises all admitted that things could not continue the way they were. The structural problem consists in an unprecedented level of world unemployment or under-employment. We are not talking here of eliminating globalization, that is unrealistic, but of how to guide it, correct it, in order to bring about greater respect for the dignity of men and women, families, nations and cultures. The decent work agenda was accepted at the Forum as a platform for dialogue, all the more since the strategy integrates the reality of globalization and the world of business and enterprise as sources of employment, but not at the price of the dignity of the human person.

The fact that the globalization of the economy is moving in an opposite and fragile direction, and that international summits are recognizing the decent work strategy as a starting point for dialogue and a recasting of the world economy, represents an undeniable encouragement for the ILO to propose decent work more insistently together with the values that it entails: that the human being comes first, that his material, moral and spiritual well-being, the stability of his family and social harmony within nations come before the stakes for profit in the dominant economic system. Promoting the decent work strategy as the basis of legitimacy of a new world economic order is at the same time a wide-ranging challenge. This perspective stresses all the more the necessity for an ethical foundation. And it is from this point of view that it is of capital importance for the decent work strategy to make reference to an ethical, moral and spiritual option that is present in the different world cultures and on which the ILO can base its policies. From the ILO's perspective, Christian references such as those found in the social teaching of the Church are of inestimable value. Being able to see a convergence between the values of the decent work strategy and those of the doctrine of the Catholic Church, which Pope John Paul II makes his own in calling for a worldwide coalition for decent work, is already a reason for hope.

But I believe it is just as important to seek points of convergence with the ethical, spiritual and religious traditions in the area of work. The question that must concern us is how the importance of work in the expectations and aspirations of men and women can be joined to the role that the different traditions can play in the establishment of an ethic of values in today's world. To this end, it is very important to see how work is understood in the different spiritual and religious traditions. It is in this context that the International Labour Office and the International Institute of Social Studies, in collaboration with the World Council of Churches, have, since last February, launched into interreligious conversation on the subject of decent work. Among the questions put to the participants representing different religious traditions were, for example, "To what degree is the concept of 'decent work' consonant with your religious tradition?", or "What are the values in your religious tradition that are found at the basis of the strategic goals of decent work?". This is scheduled to be the subject of another study seeking to show the points of convergence between these different traditions, and I list a few of these points here without commenting on them further: the positive value of work; the subjective dimension of work as a means of growth for the human person; the profoundly spiritual dimension of every kind of work, enhanced by a social, ethical and transcendental dimension. Every religious tradition represented subscribed to the decent work strategy and its goals without hesitation, even emphasizing cultural, economic and social characteristics; and certain traditions proposed the drafting of an interreligious social doctrine or ethic on work.

We have seen that a good number of the values defended by the decent work strategy are connected with values present in different spiritual and religious traditions. This can only enhance the legitimacy and firm conviction that our campaign for decent work is an effort for a just cause. Since the ILO is only at the beginning of the path leading to the inclusion of the moral and ethical dimension in the debate concerning the life and work of men and women, it is of capital importance that the Catholic Church and the other humanist, spiritual and religious traditions in the world continue to lend their assistance on this journey.

August 2002

SAFEGUARDING THE ENVIRONMENT

Dr. Eleonora Barbieri Masini*

1. Historical Context

In considering the question of safeguarding the environment, it is important to remember that, until the 19th century, the environment and all of its components — air, water and earth, that is, flora, fauna and minerals — were the prerogative of botanists, zoologists and geologists, and, in some cases, of geographers.

At the end of the 19th and the beginning of the 20th century, the field began to be enlarged to include other scientists and disciplines as well. As Pedro Beltrão, S.J.[130] has brought out, it was indeed an important moment when, in 1866, the German biologist Haekel coined the term "ecology" meaning "the science of habitat" (*oikos*, in Greek, house), that is "the environment in which organisms live and act". While still remaining, nevertheless, a matter of the biological study of what are considered the natural ecosystems, this broadened the field that today we consider to be interdisciplinary, even if it still excludes the human sciences in a broad sense.

It is interesting, however, to recall that Thomas Huxley, the father of diverse generations of specialists of the same family, presented a brief text in 1863 which refers to "human ecology" in which the human person also finds place. Human ecology will be dealt with more specifically in the section with that title.

At the same time, for several decades, safeguarding the environment and the concept of ecology remained strictly in the field of the natural sciences in the works of the great ecologists of the Post-World War II period, as P. Beltrão again notes. This includes Odum,[131] Ramade[132] and Margalef.[133] How-

---

* Professor at the Department of Social Sciences, Pontifical Gregorian University, Rome.

[130] Pedro C. Beltrão, S.J., ed. (1984), *Ecologia umana e valori etico-religiosi*, Editrice Pontificia Università Gregoriana, Rome.

[131] Eugene Odum (1973), *Principi di ecologia*, Piccin ed. (translated from the third original edition 1953), Padua.

[132] François Ramade (1974), *Elements d'écologie appliquée*, Action de l'homme sur la biosphère, Ediscience/McGraw-Hill, Paris.

[133] Ramón Margalef (1974), *Ecologia*, Omega, Barcelona.

ever, some indications of the importance of human action also begin to appear in these writings.

In 1970, Giorgio Nebbia[134] wrote: "above all, what does the conservation of nature and of its resources mean? Agricultural and industrial production, the life of animals, plants and that of urban communities is made possible through the use of the basic natural resources of the biosphere — water, air, earth, minerals — transformed into goods and services which, in an ongoing metabolism, create a growing amount of refuse: polluted water, products of combustion, solid urban, mineral and industrial residue. This refuse must be disposed of somewhere, and for the most part it is put into the same natural reservoirs from which man draws what he needs for life and production... such an extensive exploitation of such resources has given rise to the fear that they could soon be exhausted. This could impede the continuation of production and consumption in the future". This, as already noted, was written in 1970! As a result, the academic world began to raise questions from that time on.

Shortly after, international meetings began to be held. The alarm was sounded by the United Nations, and consequently by the international political world most attentive to social and human questions.

The first conference of the United Nations, entitled "Human Environment", was held in Stockholm in 1972; a delegation of the Holy See participated in it. That meeting led to the establishment of the United Nations Program for Environmental Problems (UNEP) headquartered in Nairobi. With the passage of time, it has now less on the cutting edge. Since that time, this basic theme of human environment has been promoted with various degrees of success.

Likewise in 1972, the first report to the Club of Rome was published. In Italian, its title was "The Limits of Development", a poor translation from the English "Limits to Growth",[135] which clearly has another meaning. The fact that these two events took place almost simultaneously is indicative of the increasing attention being paid at that time to environmental questions. In fact, the report to the Club of Rome, though not all of its aspects can be supported, emphasized the environmental question and the limits of natural resources. We must also mention the captivating and

[134] Giorgio Nebbia (1970), *La crisi dei rapporti tra uomo e biosfera*, Unione Nazionale Consumatori, Le scelte del consumatore, anno VI, 1 January.

[135] Donella H. Meadows, Dennis L. Meadows, Jorgen Randers, William W. Behrens III (1972), *The Limits to Growth*, Report to the Club of Rome, A Potomac Book, New York.

stimulating concept of "Spaceship Earth" expressed by Barbara Ward in this same period.[136]

This was followed by the 1976 United Nations Conference "Habitat I", held in Vancouver. It addressed the problems of living in a world in transformation. Perhaps due to the world economic and energy crises, several years passed before the publication of the Brundtland Report "Our Common Future"[137] in 1987, in which the environmental question was linked for the first time to that of poverty, and the term "sustainable development" was coined. It was widely used in a variety of ways in the following years. The report was compiled by the United Nations Commission on the Environment and Development and constituted the beginning of the discussion of the environment from a human and social point of view.

Fundamental to the discussion of the environment was the United Nations Conference on "Environment and Development", held in 1992 in Rio de Janeiro. It brought together for the first time many Heads of State and resulted in some important decisions, many of which remained unimplemented, such as the protection of bio-diversity. This meeting was particularly important because it marked the transition from the awareness of the environmental question of Stockholm 20 years earlier to the assertion that the entire planet constitutes the environment. The goal of the Conference, the drawing up of an "Earth Charter", was not attained and still has not been achieved. At the time of the Rio Conference, it was replaced by the "Rio Declaration", which was more political than juridical, a factor which constitutes its weakness. "Agenda 21", discussed in Rio and more action-focused than the Rio Declaration, also remained insufficiently implemented.

In my opinion, however, there were two positive results of the Rio Conference: the impact on public opinion, which I maintain has become stronger with time, and the visibility of women in the conservation and protection of the gifts of nature which their children need. I believe that a deeper analysis of this aspect could show that, from the time of the Rio Conference, many women, especially in developing countries, have felt strengthened in their ability to protect the natural environment.

Several other conferences followed: the Berlin Conference on "Climate Change" in 1995, "Habitat II" in Istanbul in 1996, and the famous Kyoto

---

[136] BARBARA WARD (1973), *A New Creation? Reflections on the Environmental Issue*, Pontifical Commission for Justice and Peace, Rome.

[137] WORLD COMMISSION ON ENVIRONMENTAL DEVELOPMENT (1987), *Our Common Future*, Oxford University Press, Oxford.

Conference on the climate in 1997 which raised numerous problems of a political and economic nature, as well as the Climate Conference in Buenos Aires in 1998.

There were many successive conferences and meetings throughout the world. It is well to recall here the Montreal Convention on Bio-Diversity which led to the 2000 "Protocol on Bio-Security", as well as the 6th United Nations Conference on Climate Change in The Hague in 2000. Another such Conference was held in Bonn in 2001. The debate on this question, while slow in taking off, reached its conclusion in Marrakech in 2001 at the 7th Conference with the approval of the "Framework Convention" on Climate Change.

The European Commission, for its part, has paid great attention to the environmental question, highlighting it in the Community's program for 1973 and in the following four programs. In 1986, it inserted what is called the Single Act into the community ordinance and into the 1987-1989 program of action. In Article 2, the concept of environmental protection is included. Finally, Article 2 of the Maastricht Treaty of 1993 is entitled "sustainable economic growth and respect for the environment". Since that time, the Commission has held many strong positions on questions such as the climate and the overall protection of the environment.

2. Safeguarding the environment and development. Human development and sustainable development

I consider the connection between awareness of environmental problems and the process of change in both the concept and the praxis of development to be very important. It is interesting, in fact, to note that discussion became more intense at an international level after the publication of the Brundtland report (1987) and the Rio Conference (1992).

When the discussion began at the beginning of the 70s, the concept and praxis of development were purely economic. Development was measured according to the gross national product or the per capita internal product that obviously did not take into account the inequalities at the national, regional or worldwide level. As has already been mentioned, the increased awareness of the environmental question was almost contemporaneous with the world economic crisis, related to the energy crisis of the early 70s.

It was at that time that the basic needs of the entire human population began to be spoken of [138] and, consequently, the inadequacy of development

---

[138] KATRIN LEDERER, ed. (1980), *Human Needs*, OG&H, Cambridge, Mass.

seen in economic terms, insofar as the needs of human beings were found to be both individual and communitarian. Much time was needed at an international level to change the concept of development, both considered and measured in economic terms, in order to weigh it in human terms. This change occurred in 1990 with the first "Report on Human Development" of the UNDP (United Nations Program for Development) which began to consider development on the basis of three factors that were not necessarily economic: a) the level of literacy of the people of a given country; b) life expectancy which is related to health indicators; c) per capita income as an indicator of a dignified quality of life.

In addition, the reports of the UNDP over the years also emphasized the importance of equity as regards sustainable development, that is to say that sustainable development considers the life of each person in terms of what he or she is and, furthermore, does not value the life of one person more than that of another, whatever his or her birthplace or origin. The value of development and equity for every person becomes apparent, whatever the place of birth or origin may be: Africa or Europe, North America or Latin America.

Human development is, in fact, at the heart of development, particularly in this historical moment of the international debate in which the emphasis is also on sustainable development, as indicated by the Brundtland Report, the definition of which opened a new era with regard to both development and the protection of the environment. In particular, the very definition opens new temporal and ethical vistas: "Humanity has the ability to make development sustainable — to ensure that it meets the needs of the present without compromising the ability of future generations to meet their own needs".[139] Here the temporal dimension clearly appears, that is, the need to look ahead to future generations, a vision very rarely expressed on an international level, and which involves in turn the ethical question according to Josef Fuchs, S.J.:[140] "... morality is appropriately concerned that men's various plans regarding the future — both near and distant — ensure not only a future which promotes man's values in both senses of his existence — for example in the area of biology or of technology — but a future which promotes values that insert themselves harmoniously into the whole of all the values of man, according to their hierarchy and urgency". This then is why the expression "the future of man *as* man" is so important.

[139] WORLD COMMISSION ON ENVIRONMENTAL DEVELOPMENT (1987), *Our Common Future*, Oxford University Press, Oxford, p. 8.
[140] JOSEF FUCHS (1977), *Morale come progettazione del future dell'uomo*, in: P. C. BELTRÃO, S.J. (ed.), *Pensare il futuro*, Edizioni Paoline, Rome.

In the same volume, Peter Henrici [141] refers to Josef Fuchs's text, writing that foresight, and therefore looking to the future with rigorous methodology, is not only a possibility today, but also "a moral duty". This is a rather significant expression for Christians and one that forms the basis of inter-generational solidarity. Development must consequently be human; that is, it must consider the human person as person, not just as the *homo economicus*. It must also be sustainable on the basis of inter-generational solidarity.

We will subsequently see that these concepts are clearly brought out in the Social Teaching of the Church. In addition, if human development must be sustainable and equitable, it must be so not only in terms of results but also of opportunity, possibility, and therefore of choices and decisions.

Sustainability has limits, however, which are becoming clearer with time and which pose certain increasingly urgent problems that have been well described by Denis Goulet. [142] Goulet's inquiries, which are fundamental for understanding how many questions remain open concerning the praxis of sustainable development, are the following:

"Is sustainable development compatible with a globalized economy?" An effective sustainable development will, in fact, require major changes in attitudes and politics, among which the introduction of a communal participation in the decision-making process of many governments.

"Is sustainable development compatible with a high standard of living, from a material and consumer point of view, with that being established in many (but certainly not all) countries of the world, in particular those that are called developed?" This inquiry poses another question related to the lifestyles which have become symbols of a material well-being which does not necessarily correspond to a better quality of life taken as a whole. Can an effective change of mentality, and therefore of social values, take place in both the developed and developing world? This is what Denis Goulet is asking in other words. [143]

"Is sustainable development compatible with ever greater economic disparity?" Unfortunately, it seems that the gap between rich and poor is not

---

[141] PETER HENRICI (1977), *La futurologia: perché e come?,* in: P. C. BELTRÃO, S.J. (ed.), *Pensare il futuro,* Edizioni Paoline, Rome.

[142] DENIS GOULET (1995), *Development Ethics,* The Apex Press, New York; see also ELEONORA BARBIERI MASINI (1998), *Limits to Sustainability and Equitable Development,* in: Accademia Nazionale delle Scienze, detta dei XL, Il contributo Italiano alla realizzazione della "Carta della terra", on the occasion of the 50th anniversary of the United Nations, Rome.

[143] DENIS GOULET (1995), *Development Ethics,* The Apex Press, New York, p. 132.

decreasing but rather increasing both on a national and a global level. Indeed, this increase seems to be the very opposite of human development understood in its accepted meaning of the development of the entire human person.

"How can one promote effective human development when many personal and collective interests are involved in globalization?"

"How can sustainable development be addressed without taking into account that natural resources are limited?"

These are the questions of Denis Goulet which we feel important to share and which we have developed, and in part broadened in accord with the scope of this present article. In conclusion, one can say that sustainable development has great potential if it is considered a consequence and broadening of human development, but which, in the present world in which economic forces are prevalent, also and above all at a global level, runs up against significant obstacles in being put into practice.

What is needed is precisely that change of mentality which we could call a spiritual review of the present with all of its difficulties in terms of a future which involves our children and our grandchildren, along the lines of what P. Henrici and J. Fuchs have called the "moral duty" of looking towards the future. This is the path for safeguarding nature whose seasons of growth, but also unfortunately of destruction, are long, and, as experience has shown, long-term vision as regards environmental questions is rarely found. Unfortunately, the short-term of practical economics is given pride of place.

3. Safeguarding the environment in the Bible, the Gospel (a few references and some particulars about water) and the Social Teaching of the Church

About the environment in the Bible, I believe that no better study than that of Sister Marjorie Keenan exists,[144] which I should like only to mention and recommend for reading. I should also like to refer briefly to water which, as many know, is and will be one of the greatest environmental problems. Its analysis in biblical and Gospel terms is much richer than normally thought.

Regarding care for creation, Sr. Keenan mentions numerous passages of the Bible which refer to the environment, in which, from Jeremiah 2:7 on, the Father emphasizes the importance of the care of the garden and, in Genesis 1:24, the relationship of man with creation. The need to respect the earth and to allow it to rest is also mentioned several times in the Old Testament.

---

[144] MARJORIE KEENAN, RSHM (2000), *Care for Creation. Human Activity and the Environment*, Libreria Editrice Vaticana, Vatican City.

These often forgotten references situate the current environmental problematic in the correct light. The earth is desecrated and neglected and indeed, in some cases, lost (in the sense of loss of fertility or loss of use, the effect of the construction of roads, etc.), as is happening in Italy, China and even the United States, as well as its excessive exploitation through the use of fertilizers and pesticides. These are precisely such indications that show how far present society is from the biblical teaching and how distant the human person's relation to creation is from the fundamental indications of the Old Testament.

To complete this section on the Old Testament, I should like to mention briefly some reflections of Giorgio Nebbia [145] concerning water in the Old and New Testament, the symbolic value of which, as an element of purification, is capital. For example, in the Gospel, when Jesus is thirsty, he asks the Samaritan woman, a sinner who belongs to a people hated by the Jews, for water and promises her the water of life. Water therefore has a symbolic value of purification, of meeting with the other who is different, and consequently is a sign of dialogue and peace.

These few remarks suffice to help understand how, in the Old and New Testament, the bases exist for understanding the importance of water as necessary not only for sustainability, but also for the actual material and spiritual survival of humanity. Today, more than ever, we can say that it is necessary for peace and solidarity among peoples.

The Social Teaching of the Church actually anticipated the international awareness mentioned previously, in the discussion of human development as well as regarding the consciousness of the goods of nature.

With regard to human development, we can go back to John XXIII who in *Mater et Magistra* (73) wrote in 1961: "In view of the rapid expansion of national economies, particularly since the war, there is one very important social principle to which We would draw your attention. It is this: Economic progress must be accompanied by a corresponding social progress".

In the Pastoral Constitution *Gaudium et Spes* (65) of 1965: "Economic development must remain under man's determination and must not be left to the judgment of a few men or groups possessing too much economic power or of the political community alone or of certain more powerful nations... Growth is not to be left solely to a kind of mechanical course of the economic activity of individuals, nor to the authority of government". These are truly prophetic words if we reflect upon the current historical situation.

---

[145] Giorgio Nebbia (2002), *Acqua e giustizia, considerazioni bibliche,* personal notes.

Paul VI states in 1967, in *Populorum Progressio* (6-42), (regarding the integral development of the human person): "To seek to do more, know more and have more in order to be more: that is what men aspire to now... Peoples who have recently gained national independence experience the need to add to this political freedom a fitting autonomous growth, social as well as economic" (6).

In the Encyclical Letter *Redemptor Hominis* of 1979 (15): "Man often seems to see no other meaning in his natural environment than what serves for immediate use and consumption. Yet it was the Creator's will that man should communicate with nature as an intelligent and noble 'master' and 'guardian', and not as a heedless 'exploiter' and 'destroyer'".

Pope John Paul II again emphasizes, in his 1987 Encyclical Letter *Sollicitudo Rei Socialis* (1), "the social concern of the Church, directed towards an authentic development of man and society which would respect and promote all the dimensions of the human person". Again in *Sollicitudo Rei Socialis* (34): "The second consideration is based on the realization which is perhaps more urgent that natural resources are limited; some are not, as it is said, renewable. Using them as if they were inexhaustible, with absolute dominion, seriously endangers their availability not only for the present generation but above all for generations to come".

John Paul II's Message for the Celebration of the 1990 World Day of Peace, in which he affirms that the ecological crisis is a profound moral crisis, is of capital importance. I believe that this same thought was also expressed in the articles in a book edited by Fr. Pedro Beltrão.[146]

I wanted to mention the above texts to show how far-sighted and prophetic the voice of the Social Teaching of the Church was concerning the international debate on development which, as I have tried to show, cannot be separated from concern for safeguarding the environment.

John Paul II again states in *Sollicitudo Rei Socialis* (26) in 1987: "Among today's positive signs we must also mention a greater realization of the limits of available resources, and of the need to respect the integrity and the cycles of nature and to take them into account when planning for development, rather than sacrificing them to certain demagogic ideas about the latter. Today this is called ecological concern".

In the 1991 Encyclical *Centesimus Annus* (38), John Paul II goes on to state: "Although people are rightly worried — though much less than they should be — about preserving the natural habitats of the various animal

---

[146] PEDRO C. BELTRÃO, S.J. (1984), *Concetto e Problematica dell'ecologia umana*, in: (ed.), *Ecologia umana e valori etico-religiosi*, Editrice Pontificia Università Gregoriana, Rome, p. 31-68.

species threatened with extinction, because they realize that each of these species makes its particular contribution to the balance of nature in general, too little effort is made to safeguard the moral conditions for an authentic 'human ecology'". This is the first time that the Social Teaching of the Church speaks about human ecology.

Another quotation, this time from the Apostolic Letter *Tertio Millennio Adveniente* of 1995, invites Christians to place themselves humbly before the Lord to order to ask themselves "about the responsibilities that they have as well with regard to the evils of our time".

This is a strong call to responsibility on the part of Christians concerning the various problems of humanity, among which poverty and its relation to the destruction of the environment. What stronger call could there be in the face of the difference in lifestyles from one part of the world to the other or even in the same country, or the same city?

It is also helpful once more to recall and consider the Apostolic Letter of 2000, *Novo Millennio Ineunte*, in which John Paul II reminds us "that it is necessary to ask ourselves again today the question addressed to Peter after his Pentecost discourse: 'what must we do?'".

To the degree possible, we shall try to answer this question in the following paragraphs.

4. The concept of human ecology

Father P.C. Beltrão [147] says in his fundamental article on human ecology that, from a didactic point of view, he has not found a better definition of human ecology than that of Otis Dudley Duncan,[148] according to which (the concept is summarized by Beltrão himself) human ecology is "the study of the interaction between human populations and natural environments through technology regulated by social organization".

This definition needs to be carefully analyzed in that, on the one hand, it emphasizes the importance of man's interaction with all natural environments, therefore focusing the discussion on man, and on the other hand, it recalls the responsibility of social organizations, constituted by men on principles and values chosen and shared through the medium of technology, which is the work of man and therefore must be regulated by social organizations on the actual basis of those chosen and shared values.

[147] PEDRO C. BELTRÃO, S.J. (1984), *id.*, p. 32.
[148] OTIS DUDLEY DUNCAN (1959), *Ecologia umana e studi della popolazione,* in: HAUSER and DUNCAN, *Lo studio della popolazione*, Chicago University Press, Chicago 1959.

If the chosen and shared values are prevalently *economic*, the result is technological development that is not under the guide of social organizations. I believe that this is precisely the situation in which we find ourselves in the present historical moment.

Again Beltrão specifies that human ecology analyzes all four of the variables in their interactions, and therefore not only those that are ecological in the strict sense, that is the natural environments, be they physical, vegetal, animal beings, but in interaction with population, social organizations and technology. One cannot analyze only *population* which, moreover, for Beltrão is seen not in terms of absolute numbers but of a demographic dynamic (that is, the observation of factors of increase or decrease of the population, of the structure of the population, such as the greater aging of the population in certain parts of the world with respect to others, and factors which strongly influence population trends), of human settlement (that is, where the populations are located on the territory of the planet, city, rural areas, near the sea or not, etc.) and of the professional profile of individual populations (that is, the analysis of the change in human activities from rural to industrial activities, to those of the more or less advanced tertiary sector). These modifications in the population change the relationship with natural habitats, modify social organizations, and affect the development and use of technologies.

If we observe the variable *social organization* we see that it changes with the movement of populations. We need to think only of migrations from rural to urban areas, within a continent, for a variety of reasons, or international migrations. All of these movements of populations clearly influence their way of organizing themselves socially also on the basis of changes in their hierarchies of values. An urban population is organized differently from a rural one and favors certain values over others. We could cite many examples here. At the same time, change in social structures influences the use of natural resources. It is enough to think of the need for ever greater energy sources in urban and industrial zones.

Finally, the *technology* variable exists only when linked with the choices of man and of the society in which he lives, and influences in turn the social structure that they are given through continual interaction, be it with the natural habitat or with the populations themselves in their movements and settlements.

Human ecology is therefore based on all of these interactions and is centered on man and his choices based on values which, for the Christian, are clearly those of solidarity, love for one's neighbor, and the respect for creation in view of the salvation of all.

Conclusions

I consider it important to emphasize certain conclusions of this study:

1. Human ecology is much more complex than ecology and is centered on the human person and on the society that this person builds in the various parts of the world.

2. Sustainability should be seen not only in its strictly ecological components but also in its relationships with human development and therefore in its human and social components.

3. Both human ecology and sustainability require long-term vision, avoiding the myopia of the short-term and reflecting on the fact that the seasons of nature are circular and long-term while the seasons of technology are short-term and of a linear nature. These different temporal modes contribute to the major problems relating to development and sustainability that have been addressed in this article.

4. In looking towards the future, it is important to consider possible alternatives to the present in that the future is not determined but must be chosen on the basis of truly human values. Looking to the future has become a moral duty.

5. The contribution and influence of women, as the first victims of environmental problems, in the conservation of the environment must be taken into account. We need only think of the women who gather wood for their families and who seek and transport water, again for their families. There are many examples of both the sacrifice imposed on women by environmental damage as well as their awareness of creation which gives them the possibility of giving sustenance to their children.[149]

In conclusion, it would be interesting to remember an historical moment, certainly well known to the then Commission for Justice and Peace, when, on 21 April 1967, Paul VI addressed the Commission, saying among other: "You represent for us the realization of the last wish of the Council (*Gaudium et Spes*, No. 90). Formerly, and even today, when a Church or its steeple is finished, the figure of a cock is placed on the top of the roof as a symbol of watchfulness for the faith and for the whole course of Christian life. In like

---

[149] ELEONORA BARBIERI MASINI (1999), *A Directory of Women's Groups in Emergency Situations,* WIN (Women's International Network), Emergency and Solidarity, UNESCO, Rome.

manner, the Commission has been placed on the spiritual building of the Council with the specific role of keeping the eye of the Church alert, her heart open and her hand outstretched for the work of love she is called upon to give to the world, 'so as to promote the development of the poorest peoples and to foster justice among nations' ".[150]

April 2002

---

[150] The Encyclical *Populorum Progressio*, published on Easter Sunday, 26 March 1967, announced the foundation of the Pontifical Commission *Justitia et Pax* (No. 5).

PART III

Future Prospects

THE CHURCH'S SOCIAL DOCTRINE
IN TODAY'S WORLD

Bishop GIAMPAOLO CREPALDI*

1. The Current Need for Reflectiveness and Christian Discernment

Asking oneself about the place of the Church's social doctrine in today's (and tomorrow's) world, and trying to formulate a response, entails much more than a phenomenological summary of the "challenges" that the present puts before us. It is not enough to list the "emergencies" or "priorities", nor to present a summary of the eventual "updating" that the Church's social doctrine might need. If we want to ask this question — and try to answer it — while respecting the nature of the Church's social doctrine and, at the same time, the nature of today's world, if we want to engage in this kind of reflection "from within" the framework of this social doctrine, then we cannot do without *discernment*. This is the context in which we place ourselves in order to engage in these reflections, aware that this doctrine — even in its theological formulations — is also an encounter with behaviours and needs that are characteristic of our day in general. Those sociologists who are more discerning understand the behaviours and needs that we are referring to, placing them under the category of *reflectiveness* and seeing them as representing symbolic conditions of the present existential context.

The contention, then, is that our present day is marked by "reflectiveness". By this we are sometimes referring to the situation of modern men and women who — feeling "lost" because of the rapid pace of changes and the ever widening opportunities of life, or rather of possibilities offered and paths to be taken in life — are continuously forced to "justify themselves" so as not to fall victim to impersonal mechanisms. Reflectiveness means subjective awareness in an era of a crisis of reference points that indicate the truth. It means accepting personal responsibilities in an era of great technological possibilities but of uncertain value references. No longer pushed from behind — that is, by the inertia of habits, traditions or natural dictates — nor pulled any longer from up front — that is, by powerful

---

* Secretary of the Pontifical Council for Justice and Peace.

collective goals or secular messianism — individuals must always find in themselves, precisely in their "reflectiveness", the criteria for moving forward. Modern men and women feel that the directions inherited from the past no longer suffice to define their identity, and at the same time they are almost frightened by the ever-increasing possibilities to define or re-define this identity, possibilities provided by the technology that they possess.

In other words, there is now a need for people to be aware, to be able not only to choose but also to justify their choices, to be capable of giving themselves an identity that cannot simply be passively inherited and that, at the same time, is able to withstand the enormous responsibilities that technology places in our hands. And this must not be hindered by those characteristics that, under so many different aspects, are necessary today: resilience, flexibility, adaptability to "potentialities".

The present situation of "reflectiveness" presents both positive and negative aspects. It is a positive fact that people are, in a manner of speaking, *forced* by the very dynamics of society to reflect on themselves: in a certain sense, they are called to "choose" who they will be, whereas before they simply had to "accept" who they were. On the path of reflectiveness they are more free to meet others who are involved in a similar undertaking, and above all — unlike in the past — they can do this without the oppressive cloak of ideologies. A negative fact, however, is that people search for themselves without knowing what they are looking for: this happens when individual choices are seen as an absolute priority, without taking into any consideration at all the freely-chosen bonds that have been established, even within themselves. It then becomes difficult, if not impossible, for people to rediscover themselves. When the freedom to choose is exasperated, when it is placed above every other given relation, modern men and women are forced to start from zero in the search for themselves. In the absence of criteria to guide them, they are unable even to recognize themselves when they might have finally managed to find themselves.

The individual Christian and Christian communities are likewise called to a greater "reflectiveness" with respect to the still quite recent past when social tradition guaranteed a reassuring continuity in behaviour. Between the need for Christian discernment — which is also necessary for answering our initial question — and reflectiveness, or the principal demand of the current phase of modern life, a noteworthy similarity is evidently established. It is good, however, that the correspondence between discernment and reflectiveness be understood without confusing the two concepts, because there is a difference between the field of sociology and that of theology. Giving "careful consideration to current events in order to discern the new requirements of evangelization": [151] this is Christian discernment. The exercise of Christian discernment requires *eyes of faith that profoundly enlighten reality with the freedom of the children of God*. It requires a Christian spiritual life founded on the new law of love which purges our analysis of reality of the many ideological deposits; common sense, which the life of faith does not ask to eliminate but considers a "human" dimension of our encounter with other people, Christian or non-Christian, believer or non-believer. Also, Christian discernment must not fall on our shoulders alone, but has to be "communal", taken up together with all the brethren, in the Church.

The similarity between the principal demands of modern society and the practice of Christian discernment is an encouraging fact. This latter element can respond to the need in men and women today for reflectiveness, awareness, authenticity. And at the same time it can free this human quest from being weighed down by loneliness and by the fear of becoming lost. The acceptance of a Word, the reference to a Tradition, the experience of a Community are not burdensome for the quest for reflectiveness, rather they require reflectiveness and support it, enabling people engaged in the process of reflectiveness to search with the knowledge of what they are looking for, enabling them therefore to find and to be found.

2. The Church's Social Doctrine and Christian Discernment

Responding to the question about the Church's social doctrine in today's world, therefore, means much more than engaging in a simple sociological analysis or making a list of social priorities or of emerging problems. It means making a community act of cognition, based on the reading of the signs of the times, in the light of the Word of God and of that corpus of truth that the Magisterium has constituted as the Church's social doctrine, for the purpose of guiding community and personal practices. This brings us to the very heart of the Church's social doctrine, to its innermost nature as the "encounter of the Gospel message and of its demands... with the problems emanating from the life of society".[152]

Asking what the role of the Church's social doctrine is in today's world means asking what is necessary for the evangelization of social realities: this is the task that the Pontifical Council for Justice and Peace has been responding to over the course of its more than 35 years of existence, in keeping with the mandate received from Pope Paul VI when he established it. This Dicastery

---

[151] JOHN PAUL II, *Centesimus Annus*, 3.
[152] CONGREGATION FOR THE DOCTRINE OF THE FAITH, *Libertatis Conscientia*, 72.

too, drawing from the storehouse of things old and new, continues to draw inspiration for its ideas from the Scribe referred to in *Centesimus Annus*.[153]

The Church's social doctrine is born from discernment, is itself discernment and has discernment as its final purpose. It is a doctrine that is born from discernment inasmuch as "the Church has always had the duty of scrutinizing the signs of the times and of interpreting them in the light of the Gospel".[154] The Church's social doctrine is formed in the context of a Church that wants always to "recognize and understand the world in which we live".[155] This same doctrine is then an act of discernment of the Magisterium that interprets historical and social problems in the light of the Gospel in order to provide guidelines for behaviour. This doctrine, lastly, is oriented towards discernment: "It is up to the Christian communities to analyze with objectivity the situation which is proper to their own country, to shed on it the light of the Gospel's unalterable words and to draw principles of reflection, norms of judgment and directives for action from the social teaching of the Church... It is up to these Christian communities, with the help of the Holy Spirit, in communion with the Bishops who hold responsibility and in dialogue with other Christian brethren and all people of good will, to discern the options and commitments which are called for in order to bring about the social, political and economic changes seen in many cases to be urgently needed".[156]

The importance of community discernment for the Church's social doctrine is attested to by the definition of this doctrine given in the Encyclical *Sollicitudo Rei Socialis*: "the *accurate formulation* of the results of a careful reflection on the complex realities of human existence, in society and in the international order, in the light of faith and of the Church's tradition. Its main aim is to *interpret* these realities, determining their conformity with or divergence from the lines of the Gospel teaching on man and his vocation, a vocation which is at once earthly and transcendent; its aim is thus to *guide* Christian behaviour".[157]

The discernment connected with the Church's social doctrine is therefore based on the origin, transcendent and at the same time historical, of this doctrine itself. The Good News of the Word-Made-Flesh and Risen from the dead has entered into history, for this reason history has become the staging area of our integral salvation. The dimension of the truth contained in the

---

[153] Cf. JOHN PAUL II, *Centesimus Annus*, 3.
[154] SECOND VATICAN ECUMENICAL COUNCIL, *Gaudium et Spes*, 4.
[155] *Ibid.*
[156] PAUL VI, *Octogesima Adveniens*, 4.
[157] JOHN PAUL II, *Sollicitudo Rei Socialis*, 41.

Church's social doctrine is certainly historical, but it is not only historical. This doctrine, in fact, avails itself of a light that comes from the Word of God, which will never pass away (cf. *1 Cor* 7:31; *1 Jn* 2:17), and from the truth of Christ, who is "the same yesterday and today and for ever" (*Heb* 13:8). In paragraph 3 of *Centesimus Annus*, John Paul II states his desire to "re-read" *Rerum Novarum* by "looking back", "looking around" and "looking to the future". This perspective takes on the significance of an updating of Tradition in order that it might also bear fruit tomorrow. The three temporal moments, yesterday, today and tomorrow, indicate change and, simultaneously, the permanence of the same truth.

Asking what the place of the Church's social doctrine is in today's world and tomorrow's world, as we are doing, has proper meaning only if it is placed in this theological context.

3. In the Depths of Culture: the Interdisciplinary Dimension

By means of her social doctrine, the Church "proclaims the truth about Christ, about herself and about man, applying this truth to a concrete situation".[158] It is therefore evident that, above all with regard to the future, the Church's social doctrine will have to develop more and more its interdisciplinary dimension, greatly stressed in *Centesimus Annus*: "The Church's social teaching has an important interdisciplinary dimension. In order better to incarnate the one truth about man in different and constantly changing social, economic and political contexts, this teaching enters into dialogue with the various disciplines concerned with man. It assimilates what these disciplines have to contribute, and helps them to open themselves to a broader horizon, aimed at serving the individual person who is acknowledged and loved in the fullness of his or her vocation".[159]

I do not believe that we have yet reflected sufficiently on the importance of the interdisciplinary relationships maintained by the Church's social doctrine or on how this interdisciplinary meaning becomes fundamental precisely for the specific character of this social doctrine. The interdisciplinary dimension is not something added to, but is an intrinsic dimension of the Church's social doctrine, because it is intimately connected with the purpose of incarnating the eternal truth of the Gospel in the historical problems that humanity must face. It is no accident that, in the same paragraph 59 of *Centesimus Annus*, cited above, the Pope speaks of "incarnation". The truth

---

[158] *Ibid.*
[159] JOHN PAUL II, *Centesimus Annus*, 59.

of the Gospel must enter into contact with the different branches of human knowledge, because faith is not foreign to reason; the historical fruits of justice and peace develop when the light of the Gospel filters through and passes "within" the depths of cultures, with respect for mutual autonomy, but also for the corresponding interconnections between faith and human knowledge.

The Church's social doctrine is able to pursue its task of stimulating new social, economic and political planning that is capable of placing the human person at the centre of all its different dimensions when dialogue with the various disciplines of human knowledge becomes intimate and productive. If this is not the case, there is the risk of a kind of integralistic drifting, or of reducing the Church's doctrine to a "reservoir" of guidelines to be applied to reality without mediation, which means ineffectively or even unwarrantedly, without taking into account the truth of men and women in history, alongside and together with the transcendent truth of the Gospel.

In order that the Church's social doctrine will be able to "order" the various disciplines towards a cultural, social and political planning that is at the service of the common good and of every individual, the competences of all the legitimate levels of mediation must be respected. When this fails to occur, *moralism* or *pragmatism* moves in. The former consists in seeking to apply from the outside a veneer of morality to this or that social formula. Pragmatism, on the other hand, consists in fooling oneself into thinking that it is possible to set up ways of operating that are immune to moral considerations. When one claims to draw from the Church's social doctrine abstract moralizing instructions, which perhaps clash with scientific rationality, we have moralism; when science claims to find purely technical solutions to human development and to justice, apart from the Gospel, we have pragmatism. When, however, there is deep and continuous dialogue between social doctrine and the various disciplines, we have true planning at the service of mankind. For this to happen, scholars specializing in social doctrine must be open to the sciences and dialogue with other scholars must increase: remaining exclusively within one's own group, unfortunately very common among specialists in different disciplines, must be overcome.

This concept of an interdisciplinary dimension is a theory, but even more it is a practice; it needs experts in the various fields who are convinced that it is necessary. It also needs institutional "places" where encounters and the work of interdisciplinary cultural planning can take place. It is once more no accident that, still in paragraph 59, where the interdisciplinary dimension is spoken of, John Paul II also recalls two aspects of the Church's social doctrine that are connected with this: its practical aspect and its experimental aspect. The interdisciplinary dimension aims at a planning that tends to have an effect on reality in order to transform it at the service of mankind and of human salvation.

It is hardly the case here to note how a theologically oriented interdisciplinary approach is in a position to respond to two needs strongly felt in contemporary culture and which we also dealt with at the beginning of this presentation. Modern culture rejects any kind of "closed" system, but at the same time it is in search of reasons. The Church's social doctrine is not "a closed system".[160] This is the case on two accounts: because it is *historical*, that is, it "develops in accordance with the changing circumstances of history";[161] and because its origin is found in the message of the Gospel,[162] which is transcendent and precisely for this reason is the principal "source of renewal" of history.[163] The interdisciplinary dimension makes it possible to provide orientation without being a system and to be a system without causing disorientation.

4. In the Depths of an Indifferent Society: the Interreligious Dimension

Reflectiveness, many positive aspects of which are seen in our modern era, finds itself nonetheless in a position of having to compete with indifference. In a certain sense, it is precisely this indifference that calls for reflectiveness, but at the same time it is this indifference that hinders it. This is one of the most striking contradictions of our modern era. The claim to have eliminated the "strong" foundations has given rise to the need for a greater personal awareness, but achieving such awareness is made difficult precisely by the climate of indifference with respect to the foundations, which have all been eliminated as ideological.

At the level of society, the most important aspects of this widespread indifference are the separation between ethics and politics and the conviction that ethical questions cannot be dealt with by public statutes, that they cannot be the object of rational and political debate insofar as they are presumed to be expressions of individual or even private choices. The separation between ethics and politics, by extension, tends also to concern the relationship between politics and religion, the latter being relegated to the private sphere.

---

[160] Congregation for the Doctrine of the Faith, *Libertatits Conscientia*, 72.
[161] *Ibid.*
[162] Cf. *ibid.*
[163] Paul VI, *Octogesima Adveniens*, 42.

There is no doubt, however, that other similar positions of indifference and "neutrality" at the level of politics are going through a profound crisis today: the significant recognition that religions have obtained concerning their public role is sufficient evidence of this. The picture, however, is complex and ambiguous: some religious confessions still move in the realm of a certain privatism, while others claim an immediate public role, bordering on fundamentalism. The situation has nonetheless changed noticeably with respect to a few decades ago, when the ostracism of religion within the public sector was widely practised.

It is in this area that the Church's social doctrine today and in the near future has a difficult task before it, a task that is more easily pursued if it is undertaken in dialogue with the Christian religions and even with non-Christian religions. This interreligious dimension, just like the interdisciplinary dimension, will be one of the paths of decisive strategic value in the future of the Church's social doctrine and for the good of humanity.

Looking with the eyes of Christian wisdom at the events occurring at the start of this newly begun millennium, we can identify, with the guidance of the Holy Father, at least two historical areas that are of primary importance for interreligious dialogue on social issues.

The first is found in the imposing flood of immigrants that affects the entire human family and that moves not only from South to North, as is often thought superficially, but also and above all from South to South. In his recent message for the 2002 World Day of Migrants and Refugees, the Pope has stressed how "present-day population shifts due to immigration have expanded the perspective of interreligious dialogue" [164] and he repeats that this dialogue "can translate into collaboration on common goals for the common good", [165] that is, for projects of economic, social and political intervention. Since "to be able to carry out authentic dialogue with others a clear witness of their own faith is indispensable", [166] Christians must be committed to working for the specific social goals put forth in the Church's social doctrine. This, then, is the source of dialogue and at the same time the direction and orientation of interreligious dialogue.

The second area is represented by the theme of peace and human rights. Once again, it is not the case to recall here the numerous impassioned appeals made by the Holy Father in this regard. We would need only to review the addresses delivered by the Pope to the Diplomatic Corps accredited to the

---

[164] No. 2, in the English-language weekly edition of *L'Osservatore Romano*, 14 November 2001, p. 8.

[165] No. 3, *loc. cit.*

[166] No. 2, *loc. cit.*

Holy See in these 24 years of his Pontificate to see the extensive breadth of his calls for cooperation among world religions in the area of peace, in the "spirit of Assisi". That spirit was renewed on 24 January 2002, when the Pope reconvened in that place the leaders of the world's religions in common prayer after the great upheavals following the massacre of 11 September. Here, it suffices to refer to the Message for the 2002 World Day of Peace, published on 8 December 2001, where the Pope writes: "The various Christian confessions, as well as the world's great religions, need to work together to eliminate the social and cultural causes of terrorism. They can do this by teaching the greatness and dignity of the human person, and by spreading a clearer sense of the oneness of the human family. This is a specific area of ecumenical and interreligious dialogue and cooperation, a pressing service which religion can offer to world peace".[167]

In the near future, the arenas of human rights, peace, social and economic justice, development will always be ever more at the centre of interreligious dialogue, in which Catholics will have to participate with their social doctrine, understood as a "doctrinal corpus" that inspires but is also nourished by "the fruitful activity of many millions of people, who ... have sought to make that teaching the inspiration for their involvement in the world":[168] hospitals, schools and social work bear practical witness to Gospel values, becoming places and occasions for a dialogue of life among the followers of the various religions committed to building a more just and fraternal society.[169] In his Encyclical *Centesimus Annus*, the Holy Father clearly affirms: "As far as the Church is concerned, the social message of the Gospel must not be considered a theory, but above all else a basis and a motivation for action... Today more than ever, the Church is aware that her social message will gain credibility more immediately from the witness of actions than as a result of its internal logic and consistency".[170]

5. In the Depths of the Church's Life: the Interpastoral Dimension

The future of the Church's social doctrine in today's (and tomorrow's) world will nonetheless depend above all on another element, one that is more important than the two dimensions mentioned above — interdisciplinary and interreligious — and which is the foundation of both of these. I am referring

---

[167] JOHN PAUL II, Message for the 2002 World Day of Peace, "No Peace Without Justice, No Justice Without Forgiveness", 1 January 2002, 12.

[168] JOHN PAUL II, *Centesimus Annus*, 3.

[169] Cf. JOHN PAUL II, *Redemptoris Missio*, 57-58.

[170] JOHN PAUL II, *Centesimus Annus*, 57.

to the need for a continually renewed understanding of the roots of this social doctrine in the mission proper to the Church; of how this doctrine is born of the Word of God and the Church's living faith; of how it is an expression of the Church's service to the world, in which the salvation of Christ is to be proclaimed in word and deed; and, therefore, of how this doctrine is connected with every aspect of the Church's life and activity: sacraments, liturgy, catechesis, pastoral ministry.

When the keen awareness that this social doctrine "belongs" to the Church's mission is lost in any way whatsoever, the very ability of this doctrine to express itself fully and the possibility of creating effective interdisciplinary and interreligious relationships are weakened. We end up thus giving rise to various forms of ambiguity or, in any event, to partiality. In order to engage in authentic dialogue with others, a clear witness to one's own faith is indispensable.[171] The Church's social doctrine, which "is an essential part of the Christian message",[172] must be known, communicated and witnessed to.

I would like to recall here a famous expression: "Catholic social doctrine is an integral part of the Christian conception of life".[173] This is the statement with which Blessed Pope John XXIII opened the way, now many years ago, for the successive and in-depth analyses of John Paul II: "The teaching and spreading of her social doctrine are part of the Church's evangelizing mission";[174] an "instrument of evangelization",[175] the Church's social doctrine "proclaims God and his mystery of salvation in Christ to every human being".[176]

It will be better able to render this service to mankind within the fabric of society and the economy to the degree that it is not reduced to sociological or politicized talk, to moralizing exhortations, to "a pseudoscience of well-being"[177] or to a simple "ethics for difficult situations", and to the degree that it is recognized, taught and embodied in the fullness of "its vital link with the Gospel of the Lord".[178]

We have used the term "interpastoral dimension" precisely to indicate the dimension within which the entire Church community itself must be

---

[171] Cf. JOHN PAUL II, *Redemptoris Missio*, 55-57.
[172] JOHN PAUL II, *Centesimus Annus*, 5.
[173] JOHN XXIII, *Mater et Magistra*, 222.
[174] JOHN PAUL II, *Sollicitudo Rei Socialis*, 41.
[175] JOHN PAUL II, *Centesimus Annus*, 54.
[176] *Ibid.*
[177] JOHN PAUL II, *Redemptoris Missio*, 11.
[178] JOHN PAUL II, *Sollicitudo Rei Socialis*, 3.

placed if it is to be aware of being — in the full expression of its charisms and in the integral unity of its life — the proper subject of the Church's social doctrine. Pastoral activity can be understood as one aspect of the Church's life, but it must also be understood as an expression of the unity and complexity of the whole of the Church's life and activity in the world. In this perspective, the Church's social doctrine, understood in its entire range as an *instrument of evangelization*, is not the prerogative of someone in the Church and is much more than a compendium of teachings to be used on various occasions or under certain circumstances.

The "serious" examination of conscience in this regard suggested by the Holy Father in his Apostolic Letter *Tertio Millennio Adveniente*[179] has lost none of its relevance with the passing of the Jubilee Year and with our having entered the Third Millennium. In fact, even the Apostolic Letter *Novo Millennio Ineunte* reminds us that "the ethical and social aspect ... is an essential element of Christian witness".[180]

6. Witness and Planning

Concluding this reflection on the Church's social doctrine in today's and tomorrow's world as it faces the new demands of evangelization, I would like to stress a twofold dimension of the presence of Christians in society, a twofold inspiration that comes to us from this social doctrine itself and that increasingly in the future will need to be lived in an integrated, complementary manner. I am referring to the need for personal witness, on one hand, and, on the other, the need for new planning for an authentic humanism that involves the structures of society. These two dimensions, one personal and the other social, are never to be separated. Our fervent hope is that the Church's social doctrine will help to produce authentic believers and inspire them to be credible witnesses, capable of changing the mechanisms of modern society by their way of thinking and acting.

John Paul II brought into focus this twofold dimension, personal and social, individual and structural, in his catechesis at the General Audience of 25 August 1999, and I believe we do well to recall it here. Speaking of sin, the Holy Father explained that it is always a personal fact that must not be detached from personal freedom nor disassociated from a sequence of social conditionings. Sin, nonetheless, always has a social dimension, in that "the sins of individuals strengthen those forms of social sin which are actually the

---

[179] Cf. JOHN PAUL II, *Tertio Millennio Adveniente*, 36.
[180] JOHN PAUL II, *Novo Millennio Ineunte*, 52.

fruit of an accumulation of many personal sins".[181] Sin is always personal, but there also exist *structures of sin*, specific theories about which we can read in *Sollicitudo Rei Socialis*,[182] in the Post-Synodal Apostolic Exhortation *Reconciliatio et Paenitentia*[183] and in the *Catechism of the Catholic Church*.[184] The concept of a "structure of sin" implies a "structure" that the Instruction *Libertatis Conscientia* defines thus: "the sets of institutions and practices which people find already existing or which they create, on the national and international level, and which orientate or organize economic, social and political life. Being necessary in themselves, they often tend to become fixed and fossilized as mechanisms relatively independent of the human will, thereby paralyzing or distorting social development and causing injustice. However, they always depend on the responsibility of man, who can alter them, and not upon an alleged determinism of history".[185] These observations concerning sin, personal and social at the same time, can and indeed must be understood also in a positive sense: the commitment to do good must always be personal and witnessed to by individual actions, but it must also be directed towards new planning aimed at humanizing, capable of transforming functional structural systems and not just personal behaviour. The Gospel logic of love must be embodied in the human and rational logic of the economy, of politics and of society.

It must never be forgotten that at the heart of the Church's social doctrine is the concrete human person, "man in his concrete reality as sinful and righteous".[186] The fact that this doctrine is "aimed at serving the individual person",[187] and not man in the abstract, indicates not only the ultimate object of the Church's concern but also the subject of this concern. It also indicates a method, in the etymological sense of the word, since "man is the way of the Church",[188] as we read in the Encyclical *Redemptor Hominis* and which, by no accident, is the title of the sixth chapter of *Centesimus Annus*. Who is it who will serve concrete men and women if not other concrete men and women? If men and women are true resources, as *Centesimus Annus* affirms,[189] this means also that the true resource for serving men and women

---

[181] JOHN PAUL II, Catechesis at the General Audience of 25 August 1999, 3; in the English-language weekly edition of *L'Osservatore Romano*, 1 September 1999, p. 7.

[182] Cf. JOHN PAUL II, *Sollicitudo Rei Socialis*, 36 and 37.

[183] Cf. JOHN PAUL II, *Reconciliatio et Paenitentia*, 16.

[184] Cf. *Catechism of the Catholic Church*, 1869.

[185] CONGREGATION FOR THE DOCTRINE OF THE FAITH, *Libertatis Conscientia*, 74.

[186] JOHN PAUL II, *Centesimus Annus*, 53.

[187] *Ibid.*, 59.

[188] JOHN PAUL II, *Redemptor Hominis*, 14.

[189] Cf. JOHN PAUL II, *Centesimus Annus*, 33.

are men and women themselves. This explains the need for witnesses, martyrs and saints in the area of social realities.

Popes have repeatedly spoken about those people whose presence in society is lived in "bearing witness to Christ the Saviour".[190] Among such people are those who are considered by *Rerum Novarum* as "worthy of all praise"[191] for their commitment to improving conditions for workers; those whom *Centesimus Annus* describes as having "succeeded time after time in finding effective ways of bearing witness to the truth";[192] those who, "spurred on by the social Magisterium, have sought to make that teaching the inspiration for their involvement in the world. Acting either as individuals or joined together in various groups, associations and organizations, these people represent a great movement for the defence of the human person and the safeguarding of human dignity".[193] We are speaking here of the numerous Christians, many of whom are lay people, who "attained holiness in the most ordinary circumstances of life".[194]

We must never forget that the Church's social doctrine provides principles for reflection, criteria for judgment and norms for action, "so that the profound changes demanded by situations of poverty and injustice may be brought about, and this in a way which serves the true good of humanity".[195] Personal witness, the fruit of an "adult" Christian life, profound and mature, cannot fail to be firmly based also on the building of a new civilization, in dialogue with the different disciplines of human knowledge, in dialogue with other religions and with all people of good will.

The numerous activities of the Pontifical Council for Justice and Peace during its more than 35 years of existence can all be placed in this twofold dimension, personal and social, and are directed to these two goals, the individual person, unique and unrepeatable, and society, both of which are intimately connected. These activities strive to foster the development of the Gospel potential of justice and peace both in the hearts of individual persons and in social structures. They are support activities for personal formation and are never detached from the desire to make an effective contribution to the planning of new social mechanisms at the service of the human person.

September 2002

---

[190] John Paul II, *Centesimus Annus*, 5.
[191] Leo XIII, *Rerum Novarum*, 55.
[192] John Paul II, *Centesimus Annus*, 23.
[193] *Ibid.*, 3.
[194] John Paul II, *Novo Millennio Ineunte*, 31.
[195] Congregation for the Doctrine of the Faith, *Libertatis Conscientia*, 72.

ECUMENICAL AND INTERRELIGIOUS DIALOGUE AT THE SERVICE OF JUSTICE AND PEACE

Cardinal WALTER KASPER *

I. Introduction

In the Conciliar Pastoral Constitution of the Church in the Modern World, *Gaudium et Spes* (GS), one already senses an ecumenical undercurrent in the language of the opening sentence of paragraph 90. "An outstanding form of international activity on the part of Christians undoubtedly consists in the cooperation efforts which as individuals and in groups, they make to institutes established for the encouragement of cooperation among nations... Finally, this Council desires that, in order to fulfill their role properly in the international community, Catholics should seek to cooperate actively and in a positive manner both with their separated brothers, who together with them profess the Gospel of love, and with all men thirsting for true peace" (GS, 90). Such cooperation finds expression in the form of common witness between the Catholic Church and other Churches and ecclesial Communities, so that the Church "established by Christ as a communion of life, love and truth" may be taken by him "also as the instrument for salvation of all" (LG, 9). Indeed, common witness among Christians becomes a form of proclamation of the mystery of salvation, through which Christ overcomes all sin and everything that oppresses human beings.

It is in this sense that the Second Vatican Council affirmed the importance of common witness. "Before the whole world, let Christians profess their faith in God, our Redeemer and Lord. United in their efforts, and with mutual respect, let them bear witness to our common hope, which does not play us false. Since in our time, cooperation in social matters is very widely practiced, all men without exception are summoned to united effort. Those who believe in God have a stronger summon, but the strongest claims are laid on Christians, since they have been sealed with the name of Christ" (UR, 12).

It is important to note the above last phrase that immediately establishes the foundation of ecumenical collaboration on the basis of common baptism among Christians.

* President of the Pontifical Council for the Promotion of Christian Unity.

In his Encyclical *Sollicitudo Rei Socialis* (SRS), Pope John Paul Il focuses our attention on the need for the solidarity and collaboration of peoples. Having spoken of the imperative that "obliges each and every man and woman, as well as societies and nations", the Holy Father speaks of the obligation of the Catholic Church to collaborate with others in this field. "In particular, it obliges the Catholic Church and other Churches and ecclesial Communities with which we are completely willing to collaborate in this field. In this sense, just as we Catholics invite our Christian brethren to share in our initiative, so too we declare that we are ready to collaborate in theirs, and we welcome the invitations presented to us" (SRS, 32).

These words obviously point to a spirit of readiness for ecumenical dialogue on the part of the Catholic Church as a requirement for all meaningful collaboration in the social field. This is quite in keeping with the guidelines in the *Directory on Ecumenism* that considers dialogue to be central to all forms of cooperation. "Dialogue is at the heart of cooperation and accompanies all forms of it. Dialogue involves both listening and helping, seeking both to understand and to be understood" (Directory, 172).

2. Theological Principles

Ecumenical collaboration in the area of justice and peace is a form of practical dialogue and thus needs to be well grounded in solid theological principles of ecumenism as laid down by the Second Vatican Council (cf. UR, 24). Collaboration in this area assumes that partners have already been in good ecumenical relations; that they know each other enough and have a certain amount of mutual trust before they desire to do something together in the social field. Mutual trust can also be fostered in the course of working together. Without such background, any attempt to collaborate will fail. Since ecumenical collaboration in the social field is an important step in dialogue, the principle of communion based on the Trinitarian model becomes the foundation of all ecumenical activity. The end goal of ecumenical cooperation must always be the full visible unity of all Christians. Progress towards the achievement of justice and peace will continue to be hampered not only by fragmentation between cultures, but more so by divisions among Christians. Such divisions become a counter sign of the Gospel message of reconciliation.

In order to repair the rapture in creation and restore communion and harmony, we must start with the mystery of God's redeeming work in Christ. The triune God, the Father of mercy, in his benevolent plan of salvation (cf. *Eph* 1:9), unceasingly calls all men and women to enter into communion with him in Christ's Paschal mystery of suffering, death and resurrection. In Christ, the Father has sent the Spirit of communion to the faithful. Thus the Church, which as *Lumen Gentium* has said, is "a kind of sacrament or sign of intimate union with God, and of the unity of all mankind" (LG, 1), knows that its peace is rooted in the mystery of the Trinity (cf. *Eph* 6:15). For it is God who primarily gathers together. All Christian gatherings find their legitimacy and meaning in this first call, to which it is our Christian duty to respond in obedience to faith. From this Trinitarian communion flows the Church's duty to proclaim the Gospel of justice, peace and reconciliation, to be its witness, and remind all of the meaning of stewardship (diakonia) over creation.

The Catholic Church is deeply aware of accomplishing this mission through common witness with other Christian brothers and sisters. "Cooperation among all Christians vividly expresses that bond which already unites them, and it sets in clear relief the features of Christ the servant... Through such cooperation, all believers in Christ are able to learn easily how they can understand each other and esteem each other more, and how the road to the unity of Christians may be more smooth" (UR, 12). Therefore we may conclude that the call to full communion is at the heart of all ecumenical cooperation, particularly in the area of justice, peace and reconciliation, grounded in Christ's command to love one another, to love our neighbours and to attend to the needs of the poor and the needy (cf. *In* 15:12; *Lk* 10:29-37; *Mt* 25:25 ff).

Secondly, all ecumenical collaboration must be based on the christological principle as a point of departure, because the Church's mission in the world is entrusted to her by Christ the Redeemer, who established the Church as a communion of life, love and truth. Both the christological and ecclesiological principles need to be held together in any meaningful ecumenical collaboration. That is why in *Lumen Gentium* the mystery of the Church is first of all described in the light of the mystery of Christ, "the light of all the nations", and then we read that by her relationship to Christ, the Church is "a kind of sacrament or sign of intimate union with God, and of all mankind. She is also an instrument for the achieving of such union and unity" (LG, 1). It is in this sense that the Church is called to promote that communion which is hers by her relationship to Christ. Thus the Catholic Church feels bound by this invitation of the Second Vatican Council to collaborate with other Churches and ecclesial Communities whenever it is possible to do so. This resolve has been often reaffirmed (cf. UR, 12; GS, 92 and 93; SRS, 32) and has been the background to the Catholic Church's involvement and cooperation in the social field with other Christians and ecumenical institutions at all levels.

3. Collaboration in the social field over the years

With the publication of the Encyclical of Pope Paul VI, *Populorum Progressio* (26 March 1967), the possibility and urgency for ecumenical co-operation in the social field became clear. The newly founded Pontifical Commission for Justice and Peace (6 January 1967) soon began to work closely with the Secretariat for Promoting Christian Unity in the formation of an "Exploratory Committee on Society, Development and Peace" (SODEPAX) in cooperation with the World Council of Churches (WCC). Although the mandate of the Geneva-based SODEPAX Secretariat was *ad experimentum*, practical collaboration extending to various regions of the world including joint consultations on the basis of *Populorum Progressio* were very fruitful as forums for exchange of ideas and reflections on justice, peace and development. An evaluation of this experiment shows a considerable space for cooperation in the social field despite our theological differences and difficulties encountered (cf. JOSEPH J. SPAE, "SODEPAX: An Ecumenical and Experimental Approach to World Needs", in *The Ecumenical Review*, 1974, 26, 1, pp. 88-99).

The impact of SODEPAX on the local level was far greater than one would have expected. It triggered initiatives for cooperation through justice programmes between dioceses and local ecumenical organisations. There are many examples, particularly in Europe and North America. One joint initiative at the international level is even astonishing. Despite differences between the Catholic Church and the WCC during those days of SODEPAX, both Cardinal Maurice Roy and Dr. Philip Potter issued (1973) a joint declaration on the occasion of the 25th Anniversary of the UN Universal Declaration on Human Rights (cf. "Human Rights. A Joint Statement by Cardinal Maurice Roy and Dr. Philip Potter", in *The Ecumenical Review*, 1974, 26, 1, pp. 125-127). Such an initiative would probably be too complicated today.

Since 1981 when SODEPAX came to an end, this collaboration through the framework of the Joint Working Group (JWG) has focused attention on the area of social thought, particularly on a) convergence and divergence in the social thinking of the Catholic Church and the member Churches of the WCC; and b) joint reflection on the theological and ecclesiological basis of the social thinking of the Church. In 1989, the staff of the Pontifical Council for Justice and Peace and those of the WCC Programme to Combat Racism started a reflection on the issues of racism and apartheid. One of the most intensive cooperative initiatives between the Catholic Church and the WCC was on "Justice, Peace and the Integrity of Creation" from 1986 to 1990. During this period, both the Pontifical Council for Justice and Peace and the

Pontifical Council for Promoting Christian Unity committed their staff and experts to the ongoing preparatory process that led to a major concluding Conference in Seoul, Korea, where 18 delegates represented the Catholic Church.

The Pontifical Council for Justice and Peace has always been represented on the JWG precisely in order to continue the dialogue with the WCC on social questions. Currently, within the context of the events of 11 September 2001, and the initiative by the Holy Father Pope John Paul II to gather representatives of religious leaders to pray for peace at Assisi on 24 January 2002, the JWG intends to study the specific role of the Church in questions of peace and violence. It also plans to study the Decalogue agreed upon at Assisi, with a view to finding ways of making it better known around the world.

One concrete example of interreligious dialogue in favour of peace in the Middle East was an initiative that involved the Pontifical Council for Interreligious Dialogue, the Holy See Commission for Religious Relations with the Jews, the Lutheran World Federation and the WCC Office for Interreligious Relations (OIRR). The objective of the initiative was to promote reconciliation between Jews, Christians and Muslims on the question of Jerusalem. In 1993 and 1996, the four offices cosponsored two colloquia on Jerusalem. The message of 1996 recognized Jerusalem as a "place of encounter between God and humanity and among human beings in their diversity". Jerusalem "is called to be the city of peace, but there is no peace. Although the peace process between Israelis and Palestinians has been initiated, there is still a long way to go before a just and lasting peace is achieved" ("The Responsibility of Jews, Christians and Muslims for Peace in Jerusalem, 25-28 August 1996", in *Pro Dialogo*, No. 95, 1997/2, PCID, pp. 236-238). Although the situation has become worse, we Christians must not give up dialogue, for it holds the key to reconciliation and peace.

4. A new ecumenical climate of dialogue and cooperation

After more than 30 years of ecumenical dialogues that have led to theological convergence in certain important aspects, there is a new ecumenical climate of dialogue and cooperation. Yet one finds at the same time a climate of both anxiety and perplexity as to what all these ecumenical bilateral agreements might mean for the practical every day life. This interim period in which we may speak of a real though incomplete communion among Christians (by reason of their baptism, cf. UR, 3) needs to be made concrete in the ecumenical life of ordinary Christians. What is needed during this transitional period is an ecumenism of life (witness), supported by an ecumenism of love (based on the Commandment of love) and an ecumenism of truth (in dialogue as we continue to reflect on what we have in common and what divides us). Without compromising our faith, there is so much we could do together in many areas: social witness, cooperation in the support of basic human rights, just peace in the world, the preservation of the environment, etc. Though there is awareness of certain differences in structure and methodology between the Catholic and ecumenical institutions at various levels, there has been at the same time mutual enrichment in working together with others on social issues. Such experience has shown that the approaches and methods can be usually complementary and seldom in conflict when a good working model has been found.

In his Encyclical *Ut Unum Sint*, Pope John Paul II has said that ecumenical relations presuppose and "call for every possible form of practical cooperation at all levels" (UUS, 40). Over the last 36 years since the end of the Second Vatican Council, there has been a growing awareness that Churches and ecclesial Communities must overcome their isolation from each other and together seek ways of cooperation in witness to the world, particularly on questions of justice, peace and the care of the environment as far as possible. In his first Encyclical *Redemptor Hominis* (RH) in 1979, Pope John Paul II appealed urgently to all who follow Christ to meet and unite around the one Lord. In acknowledging the need to get to know each other and in removing the obstacles that block the way to perfect unity, he said the following:

"However, we can and must immediately reach and display to the world our unity in proclaiming the mystery of Christ, in revealing the divine dimension and also the human dimension of the Redemption, and in struggling with unwearying perseverance for the dignity that each human being has reached and can continually reach in Christ, namely the dignity of both the grace of divine adoption and the inner truth of humanity, a truth which — if in the common awareness of the modern world it has been given such fundamental importance — for us is still clearer in the light of the reality that is Jesus Christ... In this unity in mission, which is decided principally by Christ himself, all Christians must find what already unites them, even before their full communion is achieved" (RH, 11, 12).

Convergence in thinking has found resonance and expression in the initiative of the Holy Father to pray for peace in the world at Assisi in October 1986 and January 2002. In the first instance, the world was facing the crisis of the cold war tensions (1984-85). In the second, after the 11 September attack in the USA, world peace was threatened by terrorism and violence. The theological foundation of the two Assisi gatherings could be expressed in terms of a gathering of religious leaders not only to affirm together the universal value of peace and harmony in the world, but more so to affirm God's gift of peace to all humanity, a peace the world cannot give. But for us Christians there is a christological principle involved in affirming God's redeeming work for the entire creation. This is realized in Jesus Christ through his death and resurrection by which Christ restores integrity and reconciliation to a broken and fragmented world. What happened in Assisi in January 2002 was tremendous common witness and solidarity in favour of peace with justice, aspects that cannot be disconnected from the Gospel of Jesus Christ.

5. Concluding remarks

For ecumenical dialogue to be truly at the service of justice and peace, it would be necessary first of all to have an ethos of ecumenism, a more positive attitude towards the other. What is needed is greater willingness to engage the other in an "ecumenism of life" through cooperation on issues that affect the daily lives of people in society. The inspiration from Conciliar documents as well as from papal documents is clear in this regard. In these documents, as we have seen, the key concept that underlies all dialogue — and for that matter the "ecumenism of life" — is that of "communio". We cooperate with our Christian brothers and sisters on social questions so that creation that has been fragmented by human sinfulness may be restored to its original beauty in the redemptive work of Christ. This task of restoration by the Church derives its nature and purpose, as we have seen, from the Trinitarian communion of the Father, the Son and the Holy Spirit. Cooperation in the social field through ecumenical dialogue therefore forms part of the search for the restoration of the unity willed by Christ for his followers.

We must admit, however, that bilateral dialogues have not yet led to full agreement on some fundamental theological questions that still divide Christians. Nevertheless, ecumenical cooperation in the social field cannot wait until we resolve all dogmatic differences (cf. RH, 12). The general rule should be: to do together today what we can without compromising our faith or going against our conscience. For this reason it is important that ecumenical collaboration be guided by the local ordinary or the Episcopal Conference, in order to ensure that all is done within the principles laid down in the Conciliar documents and in the Directory on Ecumenism.

April 2002

THE SPIRITUALITY OF PEACE

Cardinal Bernardin Gantin *

1. Peace is immense.

This means that it does not have just one dimension. It is multidimensional.

It is immeasurable in breadth, length and depth.

It is also very ancient, as old as humanity itself and at the same time as young as each generation that looks to the future. There is something eternal in peace that enables it to endure throughout the various stages of history. Its own history is quite long.

Its birth, as we have noted above, dates back to the appearance of the first man and the first woman on the earth, our earth.

God created us in a cradle of peace, making us in his own image: "Deus Pacis" (God of Peace), say the Psalms. The context prepared for peace — the peace of our souls and bodies, of our present and future — is nature itself with all its different elements, starting with minerals and plant life and including every living creature in the heavens, on the earth and in the seas. This is the first "garment" with which we were clothed and with which our first parents found themselves immediately at ease, in joy and gratitude.

2. Peace is the first flower in the bouquet that God offered to man as he came into the world. It is light, harmony, order and hope; in a word, a precious and inestimable gift.

In fact, the Scriptures say: "God saw that it was good" and beautiful — yes, in keeping with a beautiful garden, the Garden of Eden. Among believers, Catholics have the opportunity each Holy Saturday, the night of Passover, to listen to the solemn account of Genesis: it is then that we are given the clear feeling that it is in a climate of poetry and prophecy that our origins have taken root.

Everything was therefore set and ordained to confirm and to develop "the life of man", which is the "glory of God", in a universe where everything was "weight, number and measure", the first names for peace.

---

* Vice-President of the Pontifical Council for Justice and Peace from 1975 to 1976 and President from 1976 to 1984

That reality, indescribable and marvellous, is still found today in our innermost reminiscences. We are in fact well aware that without the great benefit of peace human life would become impossible, or at least very difficult, as is sadly seen in our present times of disturbances and divisions, of darkness and bloodshed. Peace and life go hand in hand.

Historically, peace, the gift of God, preceded the disorder, disobedience and revolt of mankind.

3. It seems to me that these preliminary observations correspond very well to the deepest desires of the human heart, of every man and woman since the beginning of time.

What I am being asked to speak about here is, I believe, the extent of a Reality that was first given life and incarnated on this earth, and afterwards was viciously undermined.

This is why we have received as a gift and a duty the eternal message of peace. We must first promote it in ourselves and among ourselves. This means that we must be convinced and perfectly in agreement that this is in accordance with God's will.

Believers, and all the more so men and women of every religion and spiritual tradition, pride themselves in "believing" in peace, at least as a fundamental — not subject to distortion, as we might say in modern language — and indispensable element of our existence as individuals and as a society.

4. What can we do, then, in order to live in peace? This is the burning question that humanity of yesterday and today is anxiously seeking to answer. And as it seeks this answer, humanity has before its eyes — and, without realizing it, may itself become — the soil in which the turmoil of so much violence and so many wars, each with escalating cruelty, is rooted and grows. Terrorism, which has dealt a mortal blow to peace, is the detested and unhappy child of a hatred that has skilfully and wickedly prepared and organized itself, entrenching itself among us, beginning with the mortal wound inflicted upon the seemingly most powerful Goliath of all the earth: the people of the United States of America, on an 11 September 2001 that will be for ever etched in our minds with sadness.

This terrorism, broad and formidable in extent, carries the sinister name of the devil, who is capable only of subversion and destruction by means of fire and blood. What can we do? First of all, the world must eliminate terrorism and definitively banish it, so that it will never again be found anywhere. Since it is in hearts that terrorism first takes root, it is to the depths of the human heart that we must turn in order to remove it.

No one can say that it is there that we find abstract ideas, things that "everyone knows", concepts that are repeated over and over again by the Church. It is not the Church alone but also all of humanity that must undertake this battle, without leniency and against every kind of violence, working for that justice and forgiveness without which there will be no peace.

5. In the history, the long history of peace, how can we fail to recall here some of the characteristics that have marked its course since biblical times and according to the traditions handed down for a thousand generations and more? There were once in the same family two brothers who were loved equally, both by God and by their parents, and who had everything they needed to be happy, find mutual fulfilment and grow up together; the future bode well for them. But instead it was jealousy, hatred and violence that prevailed: Cain, the elder, attacked the younger, Abel, and shed his blood. That day, peace was mortally wounded. Still today we carry the indelible and heartbreaking scars of that wound.

If at least we were able to be mindful of this at every moment, that would be a remedy for this painful and tragic memory that does not do honour to humanity. May our memory not be incurable! That was unfortunately also the "point of no return" of every sinister act to which millions of men and women were subjected, torn from their homelands as slaves, refugees, itinerants and emarginated persons of every type and suffering every misery.

These acts of hatred, which are also those of homicidal madness, were the means by which death entered into human history and put an end to the first peace, the "primitive peace". This peace, from the beginning of the ages up to our own day and at every latitude, has regrettably no longer known happiness.

That is why I experience, like many others, the surprise that I had acutely felt for the first time during the long-ago years of my priestly formation, when a passage from the ancient Roman martyrology would be read to us in the refectory on Christmas Eve: "The entire universe rejoiced in peace at the moment that Christ, the Son of God made flesh, was born of the Virgin Mary in Bethlehem of Judea". If true, that was a marvellous digression in the history of humanity! Only with difficulty can we believe this, however, knowing as we do that a fratricidal war has been raging for half a century in the very land where the Saviour Jesus was born!

6. Upon coming into "his" world and among his own, the Prince of Peace was able to give to men and women once more, if not this beautiful Christmas gift, at least the promise of joy and a foretaste of happiness. But in our day, how sadly disappointed the Shepherds in the area around Bethle-

hem would be, those to whom the Angels joyfully announced glad tidings "for all the people": "Glory to God in the highest and peace to his people on earth".

The Lord has never stopped loving us. We nonetheless await the return of a definitive peace.

I have no particular expertise for speaking here of the unending drama of that land called "holy", and which will remain for ever holy because it was there, and there alone, that two thousand years ago Christ gave his life and shed his blood for the reconciliation and peace between mankind and God, between individuals and peoples mutually.

The dimension of this new peace, "pax nova", is spiritual. It rejoins heaven and earth. And consequently, I repeat, it is immeasurable. It has to be rooted in the best part of people, of each man and each woman.

7. This leads us to consider that the breadth of peace is limitless, that peace has no borders.

Among the ideas or the ideals most generally expressed and hoped for, peace undoubtedly occupies the first place, alongside solidarity, development, justice and forgiveness. Peace is the fruit of all these values. We must add to this, in the context of daily human life, the conviction that faithfulness to our personal and social duties is indispensable. For us Christians, this conviction must be born from our faith. Does not the Gospel place at the heart of the Beatitudes, which Jesus pronounced in the Sermon on the Mount, that "peacemakers will be blessed"? That is to say, those who are determined and have assigned the greatest price, that of their lives, to the service of peace.

Jesus, who is Son of God and God himself, knows the human heart better than anyone else. He knows that this heart, however evil or corrupt it may be because of sin, does not fail to give good things to its children or to recognize in the signs of the times the fatherly and providential hand of God, Lord of time and of history.

The gift and the duty of peace spreads equally over the whole earth like the sun, the rain, the air, cold and heat, in short, like everything that forms the ecological horizon of the cosmos. If no person can live without peace, then no one must remain indifferent to the existence or non-existence of this essential element.

8. The universal dimension of peace arises not only from individual and collective responsibility but also and above all from the determined resolve of each and every person. It is not optional. Whenever national or religious leaders at any level remain deaf and indifferent to the appeals of the con-

science and of the human community and to the dictates of reason, which stand above special interests, it is unending war, all-out war that is brought about.

Are we not submerged in darkness, anguish and chaos because the dimension and dynamics of violence and war — to speak of only two of the plagues currently afflicting our sick world — prevail over the dimension and dynamics of peace? When this is the case, there is no chance for true advancement or authentic progress. What is believed to have been won on one side is certainly lost on the other. "Declaring war on peace", as John Paul II has said, means declaring war on ourselves and our own interests. In fact, it has long been noted that no war whatsoever resolves any problem. On the contrary, every country that is swallowed up in the spiral of war always brings its own problems to fever pitch. Only peace can help to put an end to poverty and misery. These are not inevitable realities. The remedy for an injured peace is an increased love, desire and effort for peace.

9. The Church does not wish to "lecture" anyone; for she has not always given the proper example herself. In fact, history records sufferings, injuries and acts of intolerance which have marked her long journey and for which she has moreover asked forgiveness. But she can neither forget nor ignore the great mandate received from her Founder: "Go and teach all nations".

Who more than the Church, and at the cost of her own blood, has emphasized the depth dimension of peace? She has explained it, proclaimed it and borne witness to it through her apostles and martyrs.

Limiting myself to speaking of the proclamation of the Gospel of peace during the past few decades, I think above all of the Second Vatican Council.

How many times the word and theme of peace are mentioned and analysed in conciliar documents, and particularly in *Gaudium et Spes*!

The Dogmatic Constitution on the Church *Lumen Gentium* begins with the words "Lumen Gentium Christus" (Christ is the light of the nations). To arrive at the very roots of peace, we could just as well say, "Pax Gentium Christus" (Christ is the peace of the nations), for peace is not only Christ's gift, but is Christ himself. He is the peace of the nations and the light of the nations at one and the same time.

Pacem in Terris, John XXIII's encyclical, is still very relevant: the four pillars of peace — justice, truth, freedom and love — retain their value as recognized underpinnings of peace.

Paul VI will draw inspiration from this to write that development is the new name for peace.

10. Cardinal Ratzinger, in a recent article on the historical worldwide event of Assisi — "Assisi, Icon of Peace", as it was so well described in the edition of 16 February 2002 of *Civiltà Cattolica* — has enriched the Church's teaching on the subject. In this article, entitled "The Splendour of the Peace of Saint Francis", he writes: "From this man, from Francis who so fully responded to the call of the crucified Christ, there emanates still today the splendour of a peace that convinced the sultan and that can truly tear down walls".

The Pope has been acclaimed by men and women who too often in their everyday lives must deal with hostility and who seem to be divided by insurmountable barriers. By dint of his personality, by the depth of his faith, by his passion for peace and reconciliation, he has virtually achieved the impossible with the charism of his office.

Certainly, the greatest and most zealous proponent, prophet and apostle of peace today is Pope John Paul II. Even as he exercises his petrine magisterium, which is addressed to the entire world, he has successfully brought together the representatives of a divided Christianity and the representatives of the different great religions of the world, gathering them for a pilgrimage for peace.

Peace and light go together. Mutually illuminating each other by their splendour, they can be described as "Franciscan peace and light".

11. The Dicastery for Justice and Peace has existed in the Roman Curia for more than thirty-five years. It is at the service of the Pope in connection with all that involves individuals and peoples in terms of rights and duties, of peaceful coexistence and of fraternal mutual aid. It is at one and the same time both the workshop and the driving force of the Church's social doctrine. We are aware of all the various papal and episcopal interventions that it has inspired. Preparations are currently being made for the publication of a Compendium of the Church's Social Doctrine. Whoever has seen this Dicastery at work or has made some contribution to it can already perceive the great impact that such a new tool will have on the world.

Moreover, it is not without significance that Pope Paul VI coupled the Dicastery of Justice and Peace together with that for the Laity by creating them on the same day, 6 January 1967, and putting them, at that time, at least temporarily under the care of a single president. The purpose of this symbolic connection was to associate with the twofold service of justice and peace the important contribution of the lay faithful who, by their baptism, are an integral part of the Church.

John Paul II will do the same by including in this service of peace the leaders of the world's great religions.

And now, after the creation of the Dicastery for Interreligious Dialogue, we stand before a new dimension of peace.

12. From an ecumenical phase with our brother and sister Christians of different denominations, peace has moved on to a simple and universal religious phase.

From its starting point in the Church of God, the Spirit of God truly blows throughout the world. We have experienced the joy and hope that this inspires everywhere.

There is no danger of syncretism or indifference if we adhere to the norms that faith and prudence have indicated up to this point, nor if our common experience is enriched by a spirit of understanding and mutual respect. Fraternal relations do not exclude the sincere and profound sharing of the same values, nor even the deeply cordial friendship that comes from the spirit and the heart together. Quite the contrary.

13. These fraternal relations, by the way, belong to that *aggiornamento* of the Catholic Church brought about by the Second Vatican Council and which finds one of its most significant expressions in the Pastoral Constitution *Gaudium et Spes*. The 40th anniversary of this document (where the Pontifical Council for Justice and Peace finds its origin) will be celebrated in 2005, and not only will it be a festive gathering or a mere reliving of memories, but above all an occasion for opening new fields and new prospects for the future.

Will the new century and the new millennium be better than those that came before? The answer depends on the future generations.

It is for us to bequeath to them the best of our hopes and the best of our contributions. If these are outstanding, there will be reason for every kind of hope.

Peace cannot wait. It is an urgent need for all people and for every time.

14. In conclusion, I take the liberty of presenting two more considerations, inspired by the great African president and poet Senghor and by the last bulletin of the international agency "Fides", which functions as the missionary eyes and ears of the Roman Dicastery for Evangelization in the world.

The former President of Senegal loved to teach that peace is always stronger and more enduring than war. It survives; it moves ahead; it always obliges people who were enemies yesterday to come and sit around the table of dialogue or under the palaver tree after wars, destruction and hostilities have ceased. This corresponds well to the thinking of another Head of State who, on a visit to Jerusalem, spoke from experience: ten years of negotiations are better than ten days of war. This is the only path that can open the way to hope.

15. Lastly, it is Archbishop Pietro Sambi, Apostolic Delegate for Jerusalem and Palestine, who wrote (5 April 2002):

"Christ's resurrection invites us not to let ourselves be overcome by despair. It invites us instead to sow, with a greater urgency, the seed of love, forgiveness, justice, peace, solidarity. A great river is the result of dozens, of hundreds of streams. The same is true for peace, with the contribution of a growing number of courageous young people from here and from throughout the world, who are convinced that peace is possible, that it is a duty and that it is the only way for achieving a better future for all".

April 2002